The Happy Mac®
Using Utility Programs

Richard Evans

Windcrest®/McGraw-Hill

Macintosh® is the trademark of Apple Computer, Inc.
Other brands and their products are trademarks of their respective holders and should be noted as such.

FIRST EDITION
FIRST PRINTING

© 1992 by **Richard E. Evans, Jr.**
Published by TAB Books.
TAB Books is a division of McGraw-Hill, Inc.

Library of Congress Cataloging-in-Publication Data

Evans, Richard, 1938-
    The happy Mac : using utility programs / by Richard Evans.
      p.   cm.
    Includes index.
    ISBN 0-8306-2471-6 (pbk.)
    1. Macintosh (Computer)—Programming. 2. Utilities (Computer programs I. Title.
QA76.8.M3E92 1991
005.7'3—dc20   91-20007
                      CIP

TAB Books offers software for sale. For information and a catalog, please contact TAB Software Department, Blue Ridge Summit, PA 17294-0850.

Acquisitions Editor: Ron Powers
Book Editor: John C. Baker
Production: Katherine G. Brown
Book Design: Jaclyn J. Boone
Cover Design: Sandra Blair Design and Brent Blair Photography   WT1

Philippians 4:6, 7

To Ron Powers and Stan Veit,
may you both live long and prosper.

Contents

Acknowledgments

The following companies and individuals have kindly granted permission to reproduce CRT screen images and material from their software manuals:

Central Point Software
Fifth Generation Systems, Inc.
Mainstay
Magic Software, Inc.
Microcom Systems
John Norstad and Northwestern University
Jeffrey S. Shulman
Symantec Corp.

Introduction

Data loss will happen. If you are going to get any work accomplished you will have to run the risk of losing some data. Keeping that loss to a minimum is the object of this book. The programs and techniques presented here will provide you with the tools necessary to keep the maximum amount of your information safe from any loss. I did not say all of your information is safe. I don't think there is a way to guarantee 100% protection of all information, regardless of the storage medium.

The decisions you will have to make as you work your way through this book will involve your time, energy, and money. Some of the programs discussed are freeware, some are shareware, and others are commercial offerings. There are strengths and weaknesses in all of them. No one will need every program mentioned. Which ones you choose and how you use them are your decision. My only recommendation is that you select and use those that meet your needs best. You also can check the reviews of the various programs discussed here for another opinion of programs' value.

Shareware developers are a special breed of user. They work hard at what they do and expect you to reward their efforts by paying the small fees they request. Unlike commercial developers their products are not sold in sealed packages. They usually are available through user groups and via download from many free and subscription bulletin boards. When you find a shareware program that meets your needs, register it. Pay the developer for his or her efforts. Users who don't register their programs are destroying their best source of low cost software.

Prepare for failures

Computer users generally fall into one of two groups: those who use computers for work and those who use them for play. There is some overlap in these groups, so not all users are covered by these labels. There is another small group that seems to thrive on making life for the first two groups miserable. These are the developers and transmitters of viruses and other types of problem programs.

Computers are machines. They are made by humans and the machines that humans make. None of these are perfect. There are weak links in the chain that binds us together. Weak links break. When a weak computer link breaks it's known as a *crash*. When a weak machine link fails it's a *breakdown*. Some of the weaker links are known and guards against failure can be put into place. Some are totally unpredictable but still can be guarded against.

Every computer will fail at some point in time, for some reason. This is at least as sure as death and taxes. When it happens, it can be the end of everything or it can be just a minor delay. Prepared users have developed plans and operating procedures that should minimize the damage done by a failure or the introduction of a rogue program into their system. These plans and procedures are the theme of this book. No single plan is presented as being The Plan you must follow. Rather, a number of techniques and various utility programs are presented, so you can make informed decisions about which plan you will follow.

Only one point will be stressed throughout: you must make a plan and then follow it. Taking your own good advice might not be thrilling, but it can keep you from having to listen to the voice in your head say "I told you so!" every time you face yourself in a mirror.

In the beginning

Until recently, magnetic media was the primary means of storing computer data. Punched cards were used before magnetic media was developed and optical disks are beginning to take up where magnetic media left off. Both hard and floppy disks store information in the same manner; however, there also are differences in these two types of disks. I'll get to that later.

The information you store on a disk is not stored as letters and numbers. It is a representation of those letters and numbers. To keep things simple only two symbols are used. They are the 1 (plus) and the 0 (minus), sometimes called a null. These symbols are in keeping with a typical magnet, which has two poles.

Getting your information onto the media is only half of the problem. In order for it to be useful, you also have to be able to read what you have written. If you only read the data and you always read it in the same manner it would be very easy. This isn't the case so something else must be added to the media. This something else is an address system. The addresses are written to the media when you initialize the disk. Both hard and floppy disks must be initialized before they can be used.

Over time, the magnetic imprint on the media gets weaker. Frequently, changed data doesn't suffer as much, because rewriting the information places a fresh magnetic charge on the media. However, programs seldom change. These files are read many times before anything changes. In some few cases, they might be the same programs that you purchased when you bought your first computer. For some users that might be so long ago that they aren't even willing to name the century. The addressing system information is the same in this respect. Once it's placed on the disk, it normally isn't written again until the disk is initialized.

As the strength of this magnetic information decreases, the possibility of read errors increases. The final result is that your system is unable to read the information that is on the disk. This type of problem can be avoided. Regular backups will ensure that all of the information still is available. Periodic reinitialization of disks will refresh the address system information so that it isn't a problem. After reinitialization, your program information also will be fresh, because you had to reload all of them.

Throughout the book, you will be reminded to make backup copies of everything. This is not this book's main purpose. The bulk of this book deals with the ways and means of preventing problems that can occur. For those problems that do happen, there are suggestions on how you can be prepared to recover. It isn't possible for me to get everything into this book. If it were, you might not be able to carry it home, assuming that the publisher would attempt to print it.

Jeff Shulman uses the term *safe hex* in his article on the differences between a virus, a Trojan horse, and a worm. It makes a nice buzz word to catch your attention. The hardest part of the whole process is making your mind up to practice safe hex. After that, it requires some behavior modification until it becomes a habit. The only problem with the safe hex habit is that, like all good habits, it is easy to justify not going to all that trouble. Not doing any number of things just once probably won't cause problems, but it might. Murphy's Law states that "if something is going to go wrong, it will, at the worst possible moment."

1
CHAPTER

Disks

The computer's ability to manipulate data far exceeds its ability to hold that data. Regardless of the amount of random-access memory (RAM) installed in the system, no data can be stored there permanently. The only data stored permanently within your computer resides on read-only memory (ROM) chips. Your primary data storage areas are on magnetic disks. Disks come in two types.

Diskettes, micro diskettes, mini diskettes, flippies, and floppies are some of the names used to describe the removable magnetic disks. Application program files usually are received on this kind of disk. Floppy disks also are one of the means employed by users to exchange information. A disk's capacity is limited (400K, 800K, or 1.44Mb). They must be considered a temporary storage means. Another type of storage means is a hard disk, which also is a temporary means of storing information.

Hard disks and floppy disks have several differences and similarities. Some of the similarities are:

- They use the same material for retaining their information.
- They retain the information written to them without the need for electrical power.
- Their electrical and logical organization are similar.

Some of their differences are:

- The amount of information that can be stored on a single disk.
- The ability to partition.
- The speed of access.

The rotation speed of the disks also is different. To understand the reason for this difference, you must go a little deeper into the theory and mechanics of how information gets from a disk to the computer and back again. The removable diskettes, both floppy and Bernoulli, consist of a circle of flexible plastic material that has been coated on both sides with a magnetically sensitive material. The coating is similar to the coating material used on audio tapes; therefore, disks have most of the same advantages and disadvantages found in audio tapes.

The fact that a diskette is labeled single-sided doesn't mean that the magnetic coating isn't on the other side. It means that, when the manufacturer tested the diskette, the second side had too many defects to allow reliable use. Those users who think they are saving a few cents by notching and using the second side of these diskettes are candidates for serious problems. When a diskette is turned over so that a single-sided drive can write to the second side, the direction of rotation of the diskette is reversed.

The inside of the disk carrier is lined with a soft, smooth material designed to trap any loose particles that might get between the carrier and the diskette itself. When the direction of rotation changes, it is very possible that some of these particles will be loosened and might ride on the diskette until they reach the read/write head of the drive. Then, depending on their size and consistency, the particles might pass undetected or slide between the head and the media. If a particle gets between the head and the media, some damage will be done to the diskette surface. The damaged surface might not hold information properly after that.

To transfer information from the diskette to the computer, it must be read. For the disk to be read, the sensitive read/write head must get very close to the spinning circle of flexible plastic. Although the present material is good and the technology always is improving, there are still limitations to the strength of the magnetic field that can be placed on a diskette. In physics, you might have learned that the strength of a magnetic field decreases exponentially with distance. (At twice the distance, the field is only one-fourth as strong.) Without getting any more technical let's just accept that "closer is better" and let it go at that.

The read/write heads of regular floppy diskettes ride on the media. The read/write heads of a Bernoulli diskette are different in that they ride on a layer of air just above the diskette. Hard disk read/write heads are more like the Bernoulli heads. They also do not touch the media. Hard disks are different from Bernoulli drives in that hard disk heads do not ride the boundary air layer; their position is fixed at the time of manufacture.

The pressure of the magnetic heads on the floppy media generates heat due to the friction between the surfaces. To limit the heat the speed of the floppy diskettes is kept to 300 rpm. At this rate the outer edge of a 3.5-inch diskette travels about 3.1 miles per hour.

$$(3.5 \text{ in} \times 3.14159 \times 300 \text{ rpm}) \div 12 \text{ in} \times 60 \text{ min}) \div 5{,}280 \text{ ft}$$
$$= 3.1237 \text{ mph}$$

An additional consideration is wear. Although the pressure of the heads on the media is very light, it still is pressure. Over time, there is a loss of magnetic material from the diskette and a little material from the head. The head material is much harder than the magnetic material, so the drive will last longer than the diskette. This wear is why it is necessary to clean the read/write heads from time to time. The softer recording material begins to coat the read/write heads, which reduces their sensitivity. Frequently used diskettes will wear first, which is one of the many reasons to keep current backups.

Hard disk construction is different in that the base that is coated with the magnetic material is not flexible plastic but an aluminum alloy or even a glass disk. The disks are assembled in a "clean" room where they are kept free of contamination. Under normal circumstances there should never be any particles inside the case to hit the read/write heads. Problems, however, can occur that were not due to particles hitting the media or the heads. Hard disks travel somewhat faster than floppies. Hard disks normally spin at 3,600 rpm; therefore, the speed of impact when something does happen will be much higher.

$$(3.5 \times 3.14159 \times 3,600) \div (12 \times 60) \div 5,280 \text{ ft} = 37.4849 \text{ mph}$$

At that speed, serious damage will occur. The edge speed of a 5.25 in hard disk is even faster.

The Bernoulli diskette is a cross between a standard diskette and a hard disk. It is made similar to a floppy but operates more like a hard disk. The media and recording material are similar to the floppy, while the speed and density of recording are more like the hard disk. There are only two sides to a Bernoulli diskette, so it resembles a floppy in that respect.

Hard disks usually have more than two recording surfaces and more than two read/write heads. The extra recording surfaces enable a hard disk to hold much more information than either the floppy or the Bernoulli diskette.

Another factor is density. Each type of disk has a limit. Floppy diskettes have either 40 or 80 tracks per inch (TPI). Tracks are concentric circular areas on the surface of the disk. Each track is further divided into sectors. These subdivisions are large enough to hold 512 bytes of information, plus an address and error correction data. Higher density disks have more tracks per inch (up to 135 or more). Their track will be divided into smaller sectors.

Floppy diskettes normally have 8 or 9 sectors per track. For some systems, the number of sectors is a constant. The Apple method of initializing, or formatting, holds the sector size constant so more sectors can be placed in the larger tracks. This method allows Apple to place 800K on a diskette that only holds 720K when formatted by an IBM or compatible. This difference is one of the reasons that the two systems cannot exchange diskettes directly. Both systems require special enhancements to read or write diskettes for the other systems.

Hard disks will have about twice as many sectors per track (about 17). They also will have more tracks per inch (up to about 600). Together with the increased number of recording surfaces, they are capable of holding many times more data than a floppy. Some hard disks are physically about the same size as Bernoulli drives, but hard drives can be more than ten times larger than Bernoulli diskettes.

When there are more than two recording surfaces on a disk, it is more efficient to do all the reading or writing possible before moving the heads to a new location. Each sector has an address. The address designations are placed in a specific way for efficient operation of the unit. The tracks that lie in the same relative position on each of the disks are called a cylinder. The tracks of each cylinder then can share a similar numbering system to locate individual sectors.

For example, this system would put sector 0, side 0, cylinder 0 at the beginning of the disk and sector 17, side 5, cylinder 817 near the hub on the last available surface of this disk set. There is another recording surface, but it is used by the hard drive unit for its own purposes, including positioning the read/write heads. A disk this size would hold about 35,000,000 bytes of information.

Part 1
Central Point Software, Inc.

2
CHAPTER

Copy II

Version: 7.2
System requirement: 3.2 or higher
Compatibility: Macintosh 512K, 512KE, Plus, SE, II

There are two parts to Copy II (Fig. 2-1). Part one is used to copy from one floppy diskette to another. The second part copies from a floppy diskette to your hard disk. These programs are copied into any folder on your hard disk or onto a working diskette. Single- and dual-drive users without a hard disk must initialize a diskette and copy the System and Finder Files to the working diskette before transferring the files from the distribution diskettes. The distribution diskettes should not be used on a daily basis.

With or without copy protection, distribution diskettes are too valuable to be used every time you want to run a program. Make working copies of each distribution diskette when you receive it. Keep these originals stored in a cool, dry, dark location

Control   Options

COPY II® for the Apple Macintosh® V7.2

Start   Stop

Original Drive :   Internal

Duplicate Drive :   Internal

Bit Copy
Sector Copy with Format
Sector Copy no Format
Track Editor

Start Track :   0   A   B

End Track :   79   A   B

Messages:

800K Copy

Copy Status

0 1 2 3 4 5 6 7 8 9 0 1 2 3 4 5 6 7 8 9
0
20
40
60

2-1   Copy II Control Panel screen

away from your computer and other types of electrical and electronic equipment. These simple steps will ensure that you get the maximum possible life from your diskettes.

The floppy to floppy part of Copy II will do a complete diskette copy without any disk swapping if your system has at least 1Mb of RAM. With less RAM, you still can make copies, but it will be necessary to exchange or swap the source and target diskettes one or more times.

The Bit Copy option of Copy II can defeat the copy protection schemes on a number of diskettes. It makes a duplicate of the original bit by bit. This means that it is unnecessary to format, or initialize, the target diskette before you begin copying. To make sure that the copy is more like the original there are two other options which can be used with bit copy.

Keep Track Length duplicates the track length exactly. This method is one of the means used to copy protect software. All systems have built-in compensation to adjust for the variations in track length because of the slight speed differences between machines. If the protection scheme involves checking the length of several tracks, these "normal" variations will reveal unauthorized copies and cause the program to fail. Some slowing of the copy process will be noticed with this option in use. There also is a slight chance that using this option will cause another protection scheme to fail the copy. You should use this option only when needed.

The Synchronized Tracks option defeats another type of protection scheme. Under normal circumstances (when the disk is unprotected) the relationship of the information between the tracks is never checked. The relationship really is not the same from copy to copy due to the various differences in machines. This difference isn't a problem because of the compensation feature built into your system. If, however, the protection scheme checks these relationships, it will fail any copies where there has been a change. Using this option also will slow the copy process somewhat.

Another Copy II option is to make multiple copies. As a shareware or freeware developer, you might find this option helpful when trying to meet the demand for your products.

One thing Copy II cannot do is make a double-sided diskette into two single-sided diskettes. When you copy a single-sided diskette onto a double-sided diskette the information cannot be directed to one side or the other. The read/write operations of these mechanisms are different. An 800K drive writes to both sides of a track before moving on to the next one.

This restriction does not mean that 400K diskettes cannot be consolidated onto 800K diskettes. It only means that any number of copy protection schemes that are on single-sided diskettes will cause the copies to fail when moved to double-sided diskettes. One way to possibly overcome this obstacle is to copy the single-sided diskettes to a hard drive first. After the copy is run from the hard disk, it can then be copied safely back to a diskette. Copy II is good and will overcome most of the protection schemes, so you can have viable backup copies of your software; however, do not expect every copy to run. There still are a few schemes that Copy II cannot defeat. If you discover one of these schemes, there are two possibilities. You can live with the situation or you can try some of the more advanced techniques discussed in the Copy II manual or one of the other troubleshooting manuals.

Copy II Hard Disk is similar to Copy II. Copy II Hard Disk is able to copy some protected programs from the original floppy diskette to your hard disk. There are faster methods of copying unprotected programs from a diskette to your hard disk. Use this utility program only when it's needed.

There are a few other cautions that must be mentioned. The list of copyable programs contains the names of the programs that Copy II Hard Disk was able to copy when it was released. If the program developers of one of these programs has issued a new version of their product, it is possible that they have changed the protection scheme. If the protection scheme was changed, Copy II Hard Disk might no longer be able to copy a program that is listed. Some developers use a protection scheme that prevents their product from working on a hard disk. Copy II can copy these types of programs to another diskette. Copying them to a hard disk is possible, but they will not run.

Be sure to make backup copies of all your program and data files. Just because you were able to copy the original from the diskette to your hard drive doesn't mean you're safe. You should always maintain three separate file areas: one for the originals you have purchased, one for your working set of diskettes, and one on your hard drive. If you do not have a hard disk, you might want to consider keeping a second set of working copies, especially true for those diskettes you use the most. Maintaining backup copies will allow you to continue working with only a minimal delay when a diskette fails. Be sure to make a new working copy before you quit each day.

If you do have two working sets of diskettes, be sure they are always exact copies of each other. For program diskettes, having exact copies means that the configuration, or customization, is the same. Having exact copies also will prevent further problems if you should have to use one of these working diskettes in the middle of a session. It is even more important to keep all copies of data diskettes current. Recovery and rebuild operations can be roadblocked completely if the information from the backup files isn't current.

3
CHAPTER

MacTools
Deluxe

Version: 1.0
System Requirement: Comes with 6.04 included on Disk 1
Compatibility: Does not support 400K floppy disks or the Macintosh File System (MFS). Rescue and Optimizer must be transferred to a 1.44Mb floppy to run on Mac IIfx, II 1c, IIsi, or Classic. Several MacTools are not compatible with HJC/Microcom's Virex INIT (v. 1.5 and earlier) when it is configured to scan floppy diskettes.

MacTools Deluxe is an integrated set of tools, or utilities, for many of the tasks you need to perform in the process of operating your Macintosh. These tools come on a three-disk set. The program distribution is shown in Figs. 3-1, 3-2, and 3-3. Disk #2

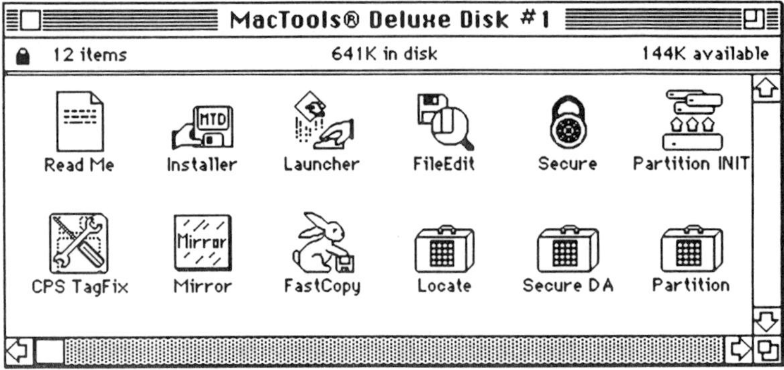

3-1 MacTools Deluxe disk 1 icon

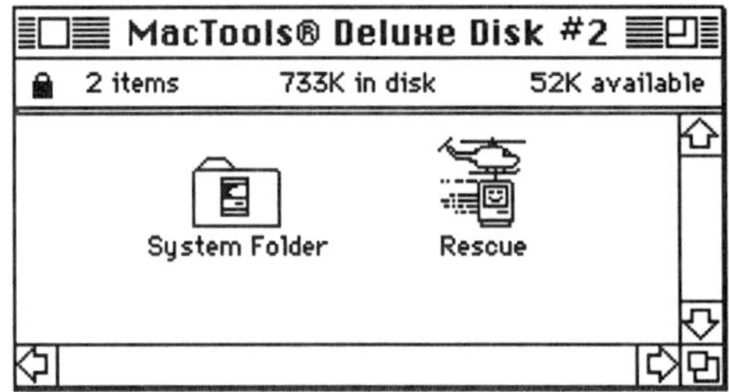

3-2 MacTools Deluxe disk 2 icon

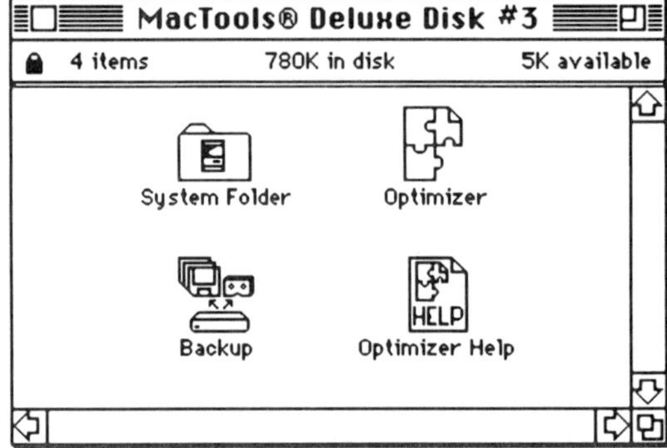

3-3 MacTools Deluxe disk 3 icon

contains the Rescue utility and a System Folder, making Disk #2 a startup diskette. You will want to be sure to have a backup copy of this diskette near your system.

MacTools Deluxe comes with an Installer program that will take care of most of the grunt work for you. One feature of the

Installer is that it will overwrite older versions of these utilities. There is no need to try to trash can the old programs before the new ones are copied onto your hard disk. MacTools Deluxe is a utility package that you should buy, install, and learn to use before you need some of its features. After you've accidentally initialized your hard disk is not the best time to learn how to use the package.

The Launcher program can act as your springboard into the MacTools world. Each of the utility programs in the package can be launched individually, as well. Mirror is your loophole in case of a crash or other disastrous happening. It is a system file that keeps a record of things. This file is located in an area that isn't usually subject to too much abuse from unwanted activities. It, therefore, is available when you need to use the Rescue utility to recover from an initialization, a crash, or a damaged file. Mirror is present on the Control Panel. You can access mirror at any time from within any application to recover a file if you have activated Delete Tracking.

The Delete Tracking feature logs the necessary information about your files to allow both Mirror and Rescue to recover them more easily. Rescue will work without Mirror's Delete Tracking installed. The process, however, will be slower, possibly less complete, and might require more manual intervention from you.

The Backup utility is just what its name implies. With it you can make the backup copies of your information and programs, ensuring that, even in the event of the total destruction of your system, you will still have your data. You, however, must make regular backups and place them in a protected location, which will not be subject to the same disaster that destroys your computer.

The Optimizer utility solves one problem but can cause another. It removes the fragmentation that occurs when changes are made to files. It also physically moves the files on your hard disk, so any free space left by deleted or modified files is placed after the end of the last currently active file. Optimizing your disk will void the record being kept by the Delete Tracking feature. If this problem doesn't worry you, you can run the Optimizer whenever you feel it necessary. If you are worried, check out the Delete Tracking file *before* you optimize.

Locate is for those who can't always remember where they placed all of the files on their hard disk. Using this utility with the file name or a portion of the file's contents, Locate will tell you the good or bad news. If the news is good and the file does exist, you can verify the contents using Locate without having to open the file or its creator application. If the news is bad you might try changing the search criteria before trying again.

The Secure utility can protect your files with a password and encryption, so only the most determined and expert programmer has a chance of getting into them. Unfortunately, you can be locked out of your own files if you forget the password.

FileEdit is a very powerful utility; be careful when using it. It is used to change the information on your disk. FileEdit overwrites data. Once it is overwritten, the original data cannot be recovered. Work on a copy, so you don't completely lose your original data. When you get all the repairs made and everything is right again, you can overwrite the original.

If you need to make diskette copies of selected files from your hard disk, the process is made almost painless by FastCopy. You also will notice that the initialization feature in FastCopy is faster than the one in Finder.

Partition uses electronics to make a single physical hard disk tool look like a number of smaller hard disks. Each of these electronic hard disks has the same features and limitations of any other hard disk. They must be treated like any other hard disk so far as mounting, backups, organization, etc. are concerned.

Now that I've gotten through the introductions, I'll show you what each of these utilities does. Do not expect this discussion to replace the user manual provided by the developer with the software. It isn't designed to do that. Some of the information presented here is in the manual, some is not. The information is designed to compliment the manual; most of what the manual says is left unsaid here.

Installer

Note: The Installer has a warning in it to turn off any virus detectors you have installed before attempting to load MacTools. There is a reason for deactivating the detectors, so please follow directions.

The Installer (Fig. 3-4) can help novice users and those who aren't all that familiar with the workings of a Macintosh. It is one of those programs that can be run before you read the manual. Installer will work properly even if you don't read the manual. Once the installer has everything copied into the correct places, you should restart your system. If you must do something before restarting, go to the Control Panel and configure Mirror.

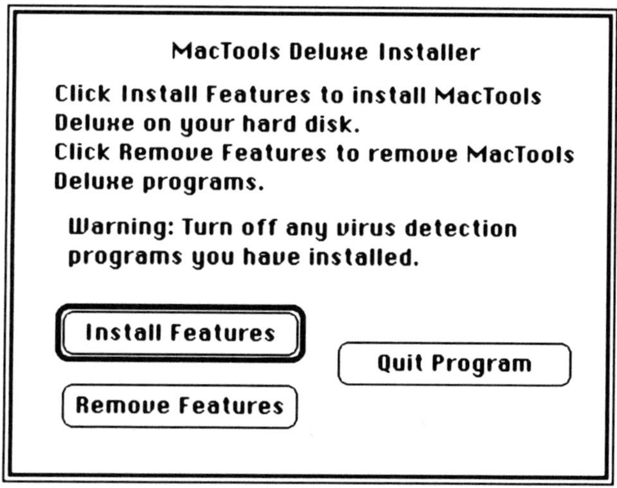

3-4 The Installer opening screen

The previous instructions assume that your system is working when you run the INSTALLER. Don't use the MacTools for the first time in a panic because your system is down. Read the manual first and perform the necessary recovery operations before you attempt to install the balance of the programs. Installing all of the MacTools could overwrite some of the files you really need to recover.

Your system should be in good working order before you copy any new software onto any of the drives. If you have your MacTools installed properly, most recovery operations will be short, sweet, and 100% successful.

Launcher

The Launcher is one way to start the utility programs. It also has some small help files attached. To launch a utility, just double click the icon. It isn't necessary to use the Launcher to start these utilities. You can double click any of the icons to get a utility rolling. The value of the Launcher is that it becomes a focus point where you can return before heading off in a different direction. It can make repair and recovery operations easier by giving you a single place to work from. Whichever way you decide to run your utilities, be consistent. Consistency will help you learn all of the features and also make it easier for you to call on the features you need when recovery time comes.

Rescue

Warning: This release of the Track Editor does not support the Macintosh IIfx, II 1c, IIsi, or the Mac Classic.

Rescue is a utility that you hope you never need but should keep handy, just in case. Be sure to take a look at the utility and its options before you have to use it. In other words, know how to recover your files before you have to do it. You might even want to delete one or two important files and practice your recovery technique.

Both hard disk and floppy diskette files that have been deleted can be recovered if you have not reinitialized the disk before you attempt to recover the files. Files on a hard disk still might be recoverable after an initialization; however, those on a floppy are gone forever after the diskette has been reformatted or re-initialized.

With the possible exception of your backup diskettes, your other floppies should not contain unique files. Your backup diskettes should be current enough to insure that there are no unique files on your hard disk either. One of Murphy's Laws states: "The probability of failure is inversely proportional to the availability of a replacement." In other words, a unique file will be the first to go.

Every recovery operation is different from the last one. A single trashed file can be retrieved without incident immediately after it has been sent to the Trash Can. Even a group of files can be quickly and completely recovered if you begin the operation as soon as the trashing is finished. The longer a file remains trashed, the greater the possibility that the file will remain trashed.

Mirror

Warning: Files deleted by PowerStation cannot be restored using Mirror.

Mirror is not one of the MacTools you will use directly. It provides the information to the other recovery utilities. Your only contact with the program will be via the Control Panel. Figure 3-5 shows the options that are available at this point. The Undelete Files option is operational only after Mirror has been installed.

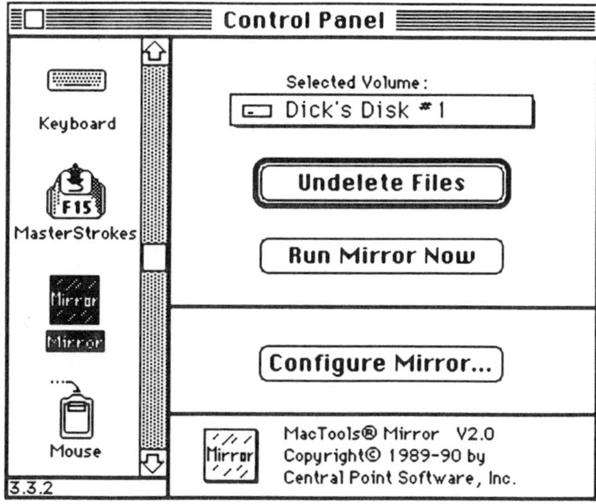

3-5 The Mirror Control Panel

The Run Mirror Now option establishes the files that Mirror requires. If Mirror has been installed earlier and the files were established, then clicking this option will cause Mirror to run and update the information in those files. (Don't worry about the time interval between updates.)

Click on the Configure Mirror option. Figure 3-6 shows the first of two screens that contain the various options you have for configuring your copy of Mirror. Notice the first option. If Mirror is going to be able to do its job, you must click the yes button.

The default update interval is 90 minutes. If you feel it wise, you can reduce this interval. Intervals of less than 60 minutes might tend to slow the system. About the only circumstance that

```
┌─────────────────────────────────────────────┐
│          CONFIGURE MIRROR        1 of 2       │
│                                               │
│  Do you want Mirror to run at regular         │
│  time intervals?                              │
│  ● Yes      ○ No        Interval: 01:30       │
│                                               │
│  Do you want to enable a Hotkey which would   │
│  allow you to run Mirror any time you wish?   │
│  ● Yes      ○ No             Key: ⌘ M         │
│                                               │
│  Do you want Mirror to run automatically      │
│  whenever you shut down or eject a disk?      │
│  ● Yes      ○ No                              │
│                                               │
│          ┌─────────────────────┐              │
│          │   More Options...   │              │
│          └─────────────────────┘              │
└─────────────────────────────────────────────┘
```

3-6   The first Mirror configuration screen

would warrant shorter intervals would be if your computer was not functioning properly.

If conditions are so bad that you are unable to work for at least an hour without a system crash being caused by outside sources, you are running a grave risk of destroying not only your applications and data but also your entire system. If the crashes are caused by program development, you might have to continue. In this case, I'd recommend that everything not absolutely necessary for programming be transferred to temporary backup diskettes. Making a temporary backup will reduce the number of programs that can be damaged by the crashes and the amount of time you have to spend getting the system back into operation.

Being able to run Mirror at will can have its advantages. Before you do something that is likely to crash the system, you can make sure that your backup is current. If you are doing program development, you could include the code to run Mirror with your work, so Mirror runs just prior to the program under development. Mirror should be updated at the end of every session. (Click on the "yes" button of the last option on the screen.) Updating after ejecting every diskette might not be necessary but it can not do any harm.

The second configuration screen (Fig. 3-7) lets you choose which of Mirror's features will be functioning. The more options

CONFIGURE MIRROR   2 of 2
Click boxes to install or remove files

Select Volume to eject:	Critical Volume Information File:	Delete Tracking File:	Auto CVI Backup:
Dick's Disk #1	☐	☐	☐

Eject   All Done

3-7   The second Mirror configuration screen

you activate, the more space on your hard disk you will be reserving for housekeeping functions. Some space is necessary, but not so much that you will limit yourself when you need space to get your work done.

When I loaded all the utilities covered by this book, got them properly configured, and let them generate their own files, I watched more than three-quarters of a 20Mb hard disk be filled with nothing but utility software. Mine, however, is an extreme case because no one will need to have all the utilities active on a single system. Some utilities had to be disabled to get others to work properly. This situation is why I strongly recommend that you confirm the compatibility of your utilities. If you aren't careful, your software could lock the system so you can't get anything done.

Although you aren't going to be working actively with Mirror as you will with most other utilities, you should know something about the program. Figure 3-8 provides a look at the informational portion of the file.

Backup

Note: Backup doesn't support network volumes.

Making backup copies of the information on your hard disk is your best defense against data loss; however, it also is about the most boring task you can imagine. About the only thing you can do is use a backup utility that will do the required work while not making it any more painful than necessary. Backup is an excel-

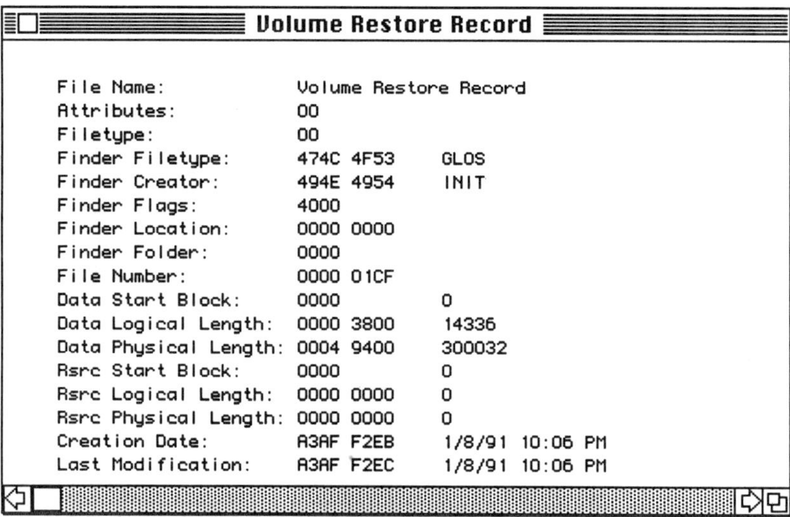

3-8 MacTools Volume Restore record

lent utility for this purpose. Its many features will help you to establish a file containing the best backup scheme for your needs, allowing you to make the necessary copies without having to remember so many details. Backup also will help you to make the copies in a more timely manner.

The Get Info screen (Fig. 3-9) is for reference only to identify the version of this utility. As you can see, it is the current version (or at least it was when I started). When you launch the Backup utility, it will do some checking before displaying the first screen.

MacTools® Backup

Macintosh™ Hard Disk Backup/Restoration Utility

Version 2.0

©1988-90 Central Point Software, Inc.
All Rights Reserved.

Continue

3-9 Backup's Get Info screen

The first time you launch this program, take your time and investigate all of the options. Be sure that you have the options you want set so your backups turn out the way you want them to.

Backup also will restore the backup copies it makes, so be careful. Users with more than one hard drive, (physical, logical, or both) will want to make sure there are setup files for each of the drives. The setup file will be identical for some drives while it will be totally different for others. The point is that you need to configure Backup to do what you want done for each hard disk.

Most backups are made to floppy diskettes. How many diskettes will be needed and how long the process will take are shown near the bottom of the screen. In this illustration (Fig. 3-10), it's going to take awhile but consume only few diskettes. It also exposes what could have been a secret; I haven't backed up this drive in awhile. I also will let you in on another secret. I'm using two systems in the preparation of this book. The Mac has all of the utility programs and illustrations on it while another system contains the word processor and the text. I've found this combination works better for me because I can look at the screens that are the illustrations while I'm writing about them.

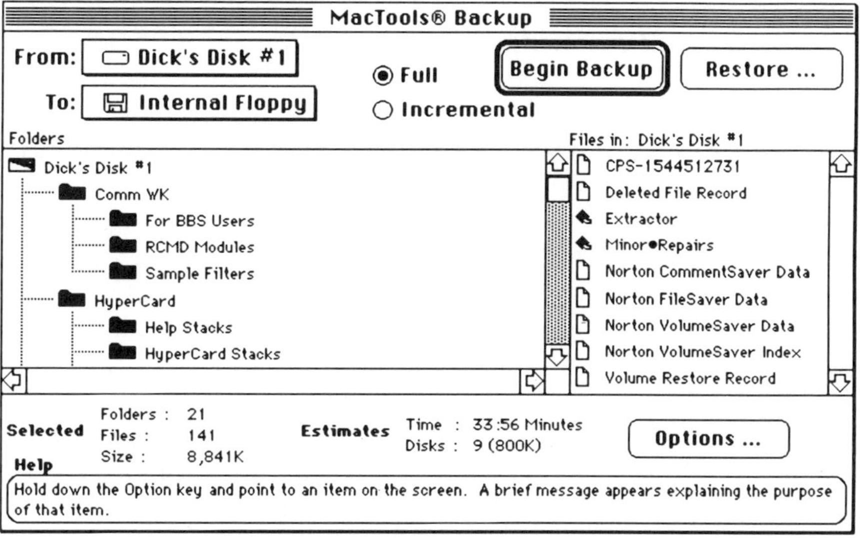

3-10 The Opening Backup screen

The Options box, when tagged, reveals a second screen of options (Fig. 3-11). The options you choose will determine how attentive you will have to be during the backup process. Compared to the estimated time required to make a complete backup,

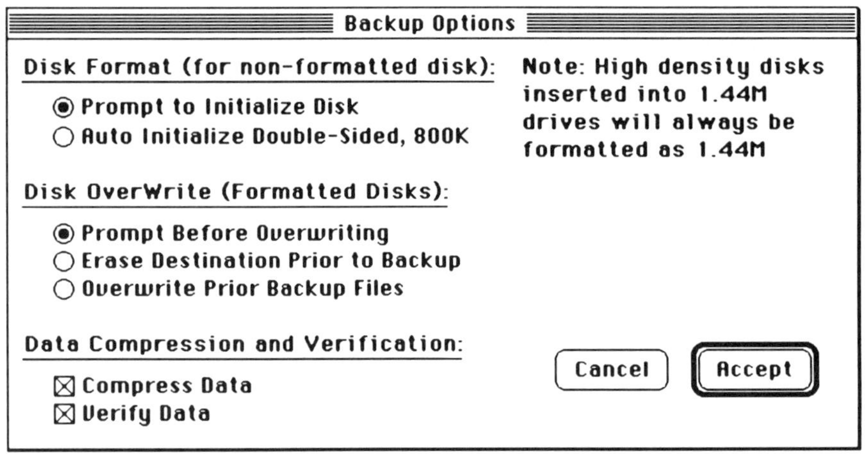

3-11 The Additional Options screen

the time for an incremental backup is only a few minutes less, with no reduction in the number of diskettes required. Opt for the most automatic process possible, so you can concentrate on other work while Backup builds the new files for you.

My habit when making backups that are going to take a lot of diskettes is to prenumber the labels. This way I can stack them up and feed the drive every time a new diskette is required without worrying later which diskette is which. If you don't label the diskettes right away and can't remember the correct order, check the diskettes. Backup numbers them, also. I use Backup's numbering as a verification of my own. If we don't agree, I accept Backup's numbers.

As soon as you eject the diskette from the drive, change the position of the write-protect tab. The diskettes were unlocked while the backup information was being written to them, but now it's time to secure that data. Your computer can read locked diskettes, so it isn't important to have the shutter in any special location when you use these diskettes to restore your files. It is important to keep your diskettes locked to prevent the accidental deletion of the backup files and to prevent you, or anyone else, from overwriting these files with different information. The possibility of an infection must not be forgotten.

Making copies of all the files in a clean system should assure that the backups also are clean. Unless something very unusual happens, the backups should remain clean as long as they remain secure. I don't think that lock and key security are required in most homes. Off-site, lock-secured storage for business files and other important information is not uncommon. The details of the security on both the system and its active files, as well as the back up files, varies with each user. Each organization also has its own ideas on how things should be secured.

Backup frequency will vary. This variance will increase or decrease the number of diskettes needed each time. Trying to keep the exact number of diskettes will be more of a problem than just setting a time/date interval for when backups will be made. Some factors to consider when trying to establish an interval length are:

- Estimated time to replace the information

- Impact of the data loss

- Amount of time and materials required to make the backup

- Reliability of the electrical source

If system reliability must be at maximum, an interruptible power supply (UPS) might be more important than frequent backups.

UPSs are not cheap. Their justification comes when the power fails. The better ones also have excellent sag and surge filters. These devices will ensure that the power that reaches your system will be the cleanest possible. Without all of the little glitches that develop between the power generating station and your computer, your system probably will experience far fewer problems. The power supplies of microcomputers are not equipped to filter out all the problems that can come down a residential power line. They are even less able to cope with the variations and problems that develop in the power lines supplying commercial and industrial establishments.

There are ways to determine just how bad or good the power is that supplies your system. Power recorders are not cheap either. If your power company cannot suggest where you might find one, the better local outlets for UPS equipment will have at least one. These chart recorders will provide you with the details of just what is coming into your system. After you analyze the results, don't call up the power company to complain. The company is charged with the responsibility of providing power and is not required to supply computer-grade power.

Most larger installations have some type of UPS. The more common type is called an RUPS (rotary UPS), which is a dc motor/generator coupled through an ac generator to an ac motor. While commercial power is available, the dc side acts as a generator and charges the batteries, which also are part of this UPS system. When the commercial power fails, the dc unit changes from a generator to a motor and drives the ac generator, while the ac motor remains out of action.

All UPS systems have batteries of some type. The smaller the system, the smaller the batteries. Many of the newer systems have gel-cell type batteries. These are lead-acid batteries, much like your car battery, that have had the acid stabilized by thickening. Large installations might have entire rooms filled with racks of clear-cased lead-acid batteries.

Optimizer

Note: Optimizer will launch automatically when your system is started from Disk #3.

The report generated by Disk Optimizer (Fig. 3-12) provides several pieces of information about your disk. In addition to having Disk Optimizer eliminate the fragmentation, I had it erase all of the free space on the disk. You don't need to erase the free space on a daily basis, but you should consider doing it after a number of files have been removed.

The actual data contained in the files is not erased when you trash a file. When the system goes to use that sector again the sector still will have information in it. If the new information does not fill the sector, some of the old information might get attached to the new file, which will cause problems. You also should erase the free space on your disk after running Disk Optimizer when there has been a lot of movement. The report in Fig. 3-12 shows that it was necessary to move 3,347K, or approximately 3,347,000 bytes, of file data to eliminate the fragmentation.

Disk Optimizer doesn't erase the data in the sectors any sooner than the system does. Those sectors that the program has

3-12 An Optimizer report

Optimizer

Tue, Jan 1, 1991 13:44:22

Volume: Dick's Disk #1

Drive Statistics:
 Drive Size: 19475K
 Free Space: 7394K

 Number of Files: 149
 Fragmentation: 3.36%

Checking: Dick's Disk #1
  Estimated Time: 8.19mins.

All Done

Checking: Dick's Disk #1
Volume OK

All Done

Volume: Dick's Disk #1

Drive Statistics:
 Drive Size: 19475K
 Free Space: 7385K

 Number of Files: 149
 Fragmentation: 3.36%

Optimize Statistics:
 Number of disk accesses: 17
 Number of blocks to move: 6695
 Amount to move : 3347K

 Avg. seek time: 56.11ms
 Time in algorithm: 12.40s
 Time to move blocks: 1.11mins.

Time to Optimize: 1.44mins.

Checking: Dick's Disk #1
  Estimated Time: 7.28mins.

All Done

3-12. *Continued*

Checking: Dick's Disk #1

Erase Free Space: Dick's Disk #1

All Done

Unfragment: Dick's Disk #1

For speed, the map will not be updated until the end of the operation.

 Skipped "System" - file busy
 Time to Unfragment: 0.71mins.

All Done

freed still could contain all or part of some of the files that have just been defragmented; they could become a problem. Another reason for erasing free space is the matter of cross-linking. When all of the free space really is empty, the system should not be able to cross-link files as it writes them to the disk.

Users who are required to relocate files on their disks regularly should use both the erase empty space and defragment options of Disk Optimizer at regular intervals. Erasing empty space after defragmenting might make the recovery of a file that has been trashed for any length of time much more difficult; however, it will make recovering all of the current files much easier. It also will keep your system running closer to its optimum performance level.

Locate

The example shown in Fig. 3-13 is a simple one. Although no filename is shown, the keyword *Delphi* should be found in a number of files.

Delphi is also a part of the word Phila*delphi*a, which is one of the words that Locate accepted as meeting the search criteria. Each of the files listed in the Fig. 3-14 includes a word containing the string *delphi*. The elevator bar on the right side of the listing is hatched, indicating that there are more files in the listing than are displayed in the window.

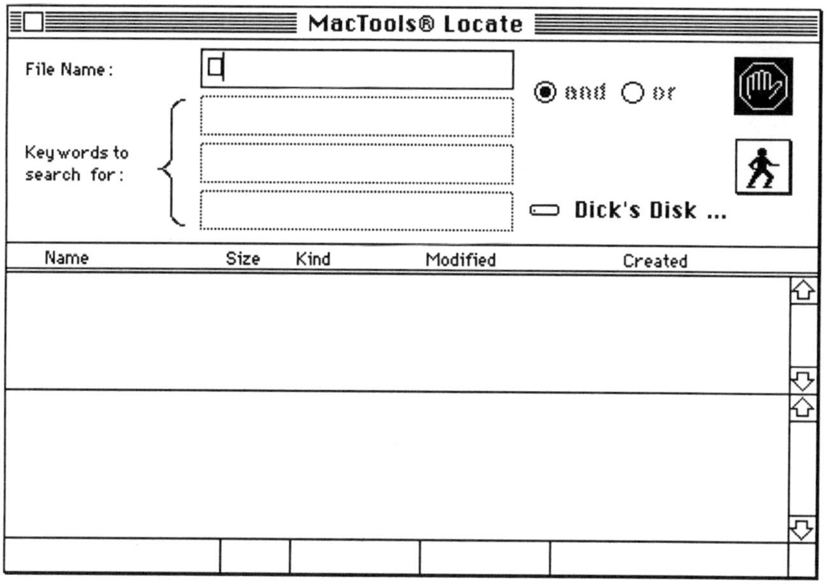

3-13 The MacTools Locate screen

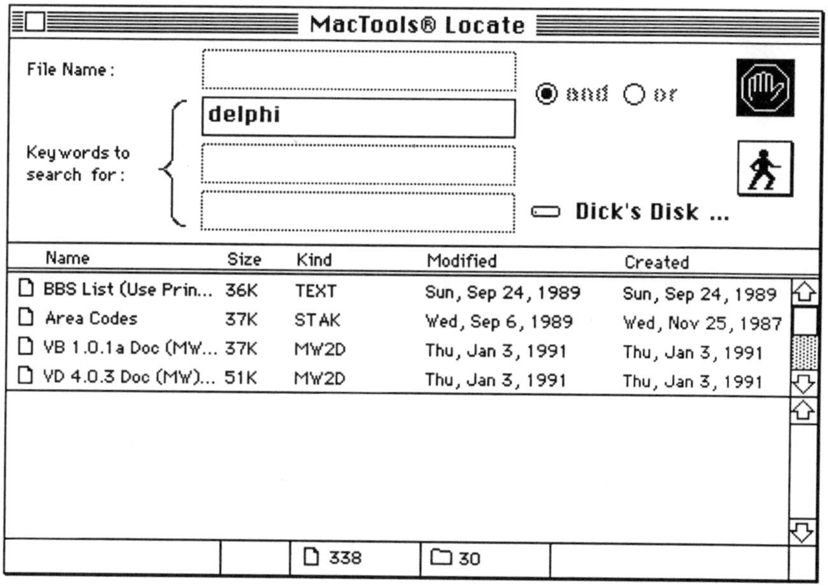

3-14 The same screen after Locate found things

Locate has found those files with the correct word in them (see Fig. 3-15). With the information shown in the upper and lower window, you will know which file you're looking for and how to access it. Using Locate might not be the fastest possible way to find something in a file, but it's a lot faster than having to open and read every file to find what you're looking for.

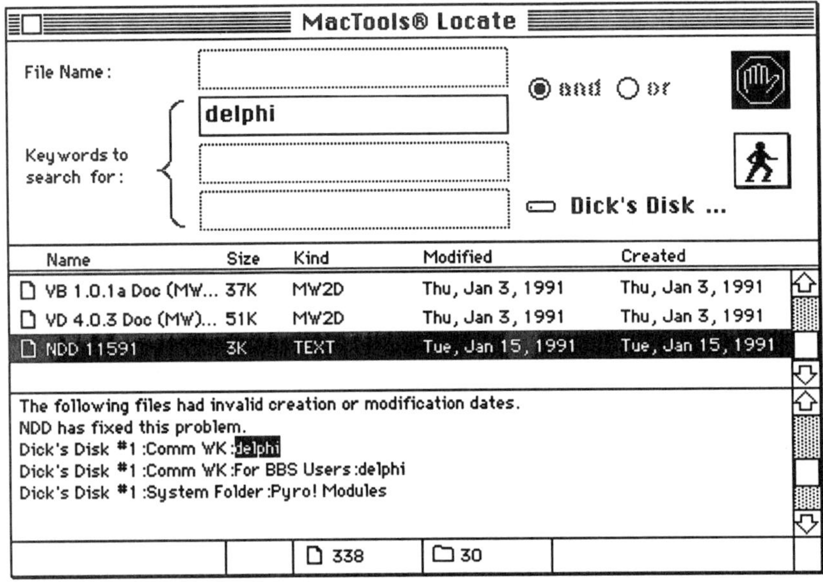

3-15 Looking at a *delphi* in a file

You can help Locate to work faster by giving it smaller sections of the disk to search. (You can use Partition to divide the disk.) You also can supply more specific search criteria. This example was vague for the purpose of illustration, not as a true example of the power and usefulness of this utility.

Secure

Note: The Secure utility is restricted by Federal Law to U.S. and Canadian distribution only.

The Secure utility program provides three features that will help you protect your sensitive files. First, you can encrypt the files. Encryption is another word for encoding. The clear code or text of your file is translated into another format using different characters to represent your information. A key word is required for this feature. If the key word is lost, consider the data lost.

The compression feature reduces file size as much as 60%. Files cannot run in this format, but they can be transmitted via disk or modem for decompression and use by another user. When using a modem, reduced file size will reduce your phone bill, bulletin board service connect time bill, or both. If you are using diskettes to exchange information, more compressed files will fit on a diskette, saving diskette costs as well as postage. If the compressed files are lost, they might not be of any use to whoever finds them. A copy of MacTools Deluxe will be necessary to decompress them.

Password protection can work; however, using a word like "password" as the password to protect your sensitive information is a useless exercise in frustration. The same can be said of the words "confidential" and "private." All of these have been found by security consultants and inspectors as the real passwords protecting truly sensitive information. The better passwords are random alphanumeric mixtures at least 6 characters long. Strings of 10 to 12 characters will increase the cracking difficulty. The longer string, however, also is harder for you to remember, which leads to the next most common breach of security.

Putting the password on a sticky note and pasting it on the monitor completely negates the security system. The same goes for putting it under the keyboard. Writing the password in any place that does not remain under your control at all times can cause a breach. Just writing down your password can be a breach of security with some systems. If you must write down your password until you can memorize it, keep the piece of paper on your person at all times. (The usual exceptions apply at home.) Never leave your password laying around the office for any reason at any time. In some organizations, any lapse in computer security can be hazardous to your job security.

Be sure to observe the rules for generating passwords, too. In places where security is very strict, the rules will be strict, as well. The lock, or password, being devised need only be as strong as the need to keep dishonest people in the area from accessing the data. No lock yet devised will keep a determined thief out. Where one technique won't work, another one is tried until the lock is finally broken.

Security is improved by keeping the passwords relatively new. Breaking any good password takes time. Once a password is broken, it can be useful as a pattern for future passwords. If the new passwords do not follow that pattern, then the thief must take the same time-consuming steps to break the new password. This type of frustration might convince the thief to look elsewhere for data to steal.

FileEdit

FileEdit can be a helpful and powerful utility. If it is not used properly, however, it can terminate your access to your disks and corrupt your data to the point that the data becomes useless.

FileEdit gives you access to everything on your hard disk, including the files you knew were there but couldn't find as well as those you could see but couldn't touch. For recovery and repair operations, FileEdit is the tool to use.

Be careful when using FileEdit. All of the safeties built into this program can be overridden. Any mistakes you make can easily become permanent. You also can cause yourself a lot of expensive grief.

If you know how to read the data on your disks and know where to make changes, you will appreciate the ease with which you can find the addresses that need changing. Although the FileEdit utility will increase the speed of recovery operations, they probably will not be short and sweet. Patience and strict attention to every detail is the only way to gain the most from any recovery attempt.

A few losses also will brand your errors into your brain forever; however, I don't recommend learning by loss or error. Those of you who have never lost a byte soon will join in the ranks of those who have lost and recovered data as well as those who have lost data and still not recovered it.

FastCopy

Warning: This release of the Track Editor does not support the Macintosh IIfx, II 1c, IIsi, or the Mac Classic.

As indicated by the Opening Screen (Fig. 3-16), there is more to FastCopy than just the ability to copy diskettes. All of these

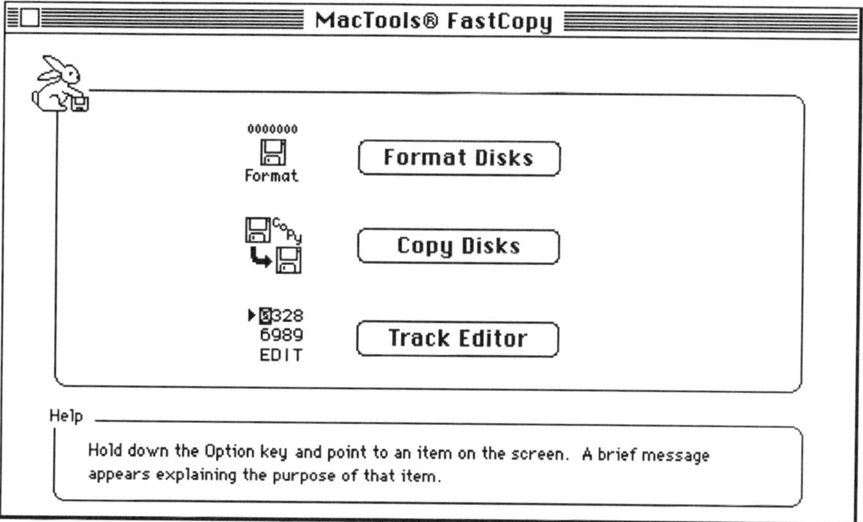

3-16 The FastCopy opening screen

utilities are diskette programs. Even before copying is listed, the format, or initialization, feature is presented. The Track Editor allows you access to all of the data on your diskettes. You should study this feature and use it only when necessary. Like any other powerful tool, the Track Editor can cause serious damage if it is misused.

This version of MacTools is compatible with the newer high-density diskettes and drives. If your system has a new drive, both of the option buttons will have dark outlines, with the center filled on the one you have selected. The utility will default to the 1.44Mb option if a high-density drive is present; otherwise it will default to the 800K option (Fig. 3-17). The diskette markings are easily read on the metal slide. The double-density, or 800K, diskettes are marked as MFD-2DD, while the high-density, or 1.44Mb, diskettes are marked MF-2HD. You can format a high-density diskette as an 800K diskette; however, it is not recommended. Double-density, or 800K, diskettes cannot be formatted to 1.44Mb. If the error traps of the software do not prevent you from formatting an 800K diskette using the 1.44Mb format, your system will. The system prevents you from formatting double-density diskettes at high-density because they will not be able to be read by any type of drive.

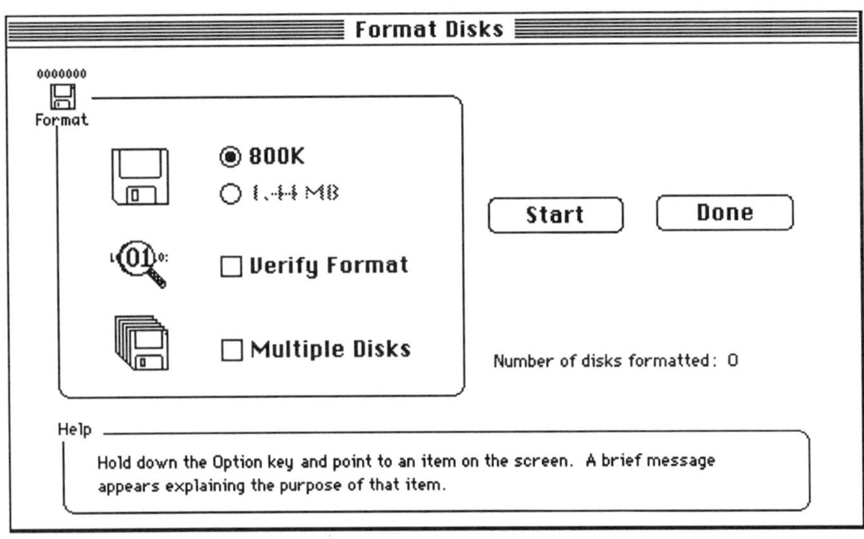

3-17 FastCopy's Format Disks option

If the other options are marked, FastCopy will format more than a single diskette. Verification might not be necessary every time you format a diskette. Verification takes time and usually doesn't find anything because the format is usually correct. If sensitive data is to be placed on the diskette, the extra time needed to verify the diskette is well worth the investment. Fast-Copy doesn't usually miss problems in the making (like bad sectors) when formatting. Having a little insurance for special diskettes isn't being excessive; however, a lack of it will come back to haunt you if there is a problem.

There are several options available when copying. In addition to being able to make more than one copy of any diskette, there is an option to copy the used sectors only. Using this option will make copying much quicker if not all of the sectors are in use. Options to verify the diskette and to format before copying are available. The other options are available when you change the To: and From: internal/image, or source and target locations. Figure 3-18 is a representation of the screen. An image file is one that was on a floppy and now is on your hard drive. It has been placed there as the source for making multiple copies.

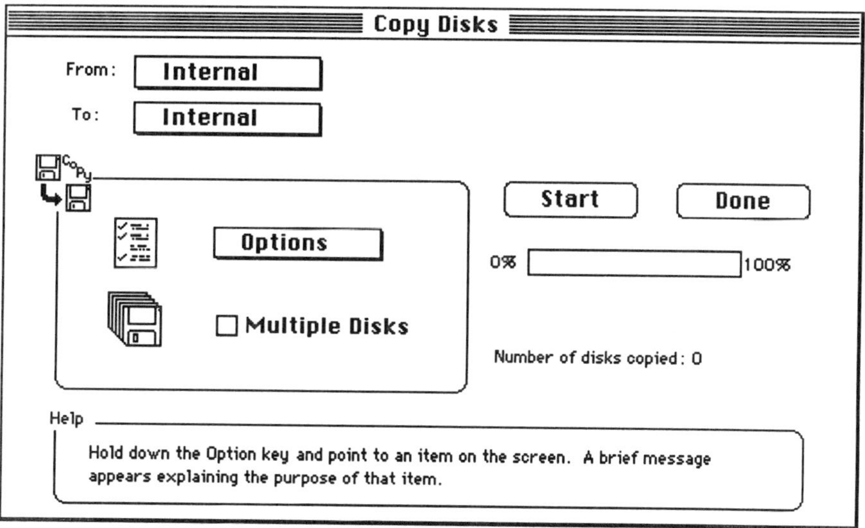

3-18 FastCopy's Copy Disks screen

Track Editor

Note: This version of Track Editor doesn't support 1.44Mb diskettes.

The Track Editor isn't FileEdit; however, some editing capabilities are shared by both. (Figure 3-19 is a typical Track Editor screen.) The differences between the two utilities appears when you go looking for specifics. The FileEdit editor works with blocks of information on your disk, while the Track Editor works with individual tracks. Track Editor will edit the tracks on both hard and floppy disks. Another difference is that you do not launch the Track Editor using the Launcher. To start the Track Editor you first must have launched Rescue or FastCopy.

Editing by bytes is not a quick process, nor is it one to be started without fully knowing what you are doing. If you must experiment, do it with a copy of some noncritical data. This experimenting will enable you to change things so you can better understand how to make changes when the need arises.

Track Editor is a recovery tool, while FileEdit is more a management tool. You can do other things with FileEdit; however, the only function of Track Edit is to make changes to the data on your disks, byte by byte.

```
≣□ ≣≣≣≣≣≣≣≣≣≣≣≣≣≣≣≣≣≣ Track Editor ≣≣≣≣≣≣≣≣≣≣
⌂ Vol:VirusDetective ... Size:800K  Drv:Internal          Spd:8mHz
0000:  9A B4 B4 B4 B4 B4 B4 B4 B4 B4 B4 B4 B4 B4 B4 B4    ⬆   Track: 0
0010:  B4 B4 B4 B4 B4 B4 B4 B4 B4 B4 B4 B4 B4 B4 B4 B4        Side:A
0020:  B4 B4 B4 B4 B4 B4 B4 B4 B4 B4 B4 B4 B4 B4 B4 B4
0030:  B4 B4 B4 B4 B4 B4 B4 B4 B4 B4 B4 B4 B4 B4 B4 B4        Track
0040:  B4 B4 B4 B4 B4 B4 B4 B4 B4 B4 B4 B4 B4 B4 B4 B4        Length:
0050:  B4 B4 B4 B4 B4 B4 B4 B4 B4 B4 B4 B4 B4 B4 B4 B4        0
0060:  B4 B4 B4 B4 B4 B4 B4 B4 B4 B4 B4 B4 B4 B4 B4 B4
0070:  B4 B4 B4 B4 B4 B4 B4 B4 B4 B4 B4 B4 B4 B4 B4 B4        Track
0080:  B4 B4 B4 B4 B4 B4 B4 B4 B4 B4 B4 B4 B4 B4 B4 B4        Start:
0090:  B4 B4 B4 B4 B4 B4 B4 B4 B4 B4 B4 B4 B4 B4 B4 B4        0000
00A0:  B4 B4 B4 B4 B4 B4 B4 B4 B4 B4 B4 B4 B4 B4 B4 B4        Track
00B0:  B4 B4 B4 B4 B4 B4 B4 B4 B4 B4 B4 B4 B4 B4 B4 B4        End:
00C0:  B4 B4 B4 B4 B4 B4 B4 B4 B4 B4 B4 B4 B4 B4 B4 B4        7130
00D0:  B4 B4 B4 B4 B4 B4 B4 B4 B4 B4 B4 B4 B4 B4 B4 B4        Write
00E0:  B4 B4 B4 B4 B4 B4 B4 B4 B4 B4 B4 B4 B4 B4 B4 B4        Track
00F0:  B4 B4 B4 B4 B4 B4 B4 B4 B4 B4 B4 B4 B4 B4 B4 B4    ⬇   From:
                                                              0000
```

3-19 MacTools Track Editor screen

You should know how to use the recovery tools in this package before you are required to use them. If you don't plan ahead and must use the tools before you have experimented with them, then you must read the manual before attempting byte by byte recovery or repair. Here, too, if it's possible to work on a copy rather than the original data, do so. This way, you can try again if you fail to solve the problem.

On the screen, information about the data's location surrounds the actual data. The volume name, disk size, drive location, and processor speed are shown at the top. Down the right-hand side of the screen are the major items. The left-hand side shows the beginning address of the bytes in that line. They read from left to right and from 0 to F. The addresses shown are all decimal numbers; however, the hex portions of these addresses will appear later as you scroll deeper into the information.

To fully utilize the information shown by the Track Editor you will need to refer to the Look-up Table in the Technical Notes portion of your software manual. You also will have to know what you are doing before you start making changes with this utility. Editing here means overwriting the existing information.

One side effect of making changes with the Track Editor is that the changes will make the checksum incorrect. Before the file is fully ready to run again, the checksum will need to be recalculated. The Track Editor has the necessary features to be able to perform this corrective action. The former information cannot be recovered. For this reason, you should be working on a copy of the file rather than the original. If you make a change that ends up creating more problems than it solves, you can trash that copy and start again with another copy. If you make a mistake while working on the original, you will have lost any means of repairing the file.

Don't attempt to use the Track Editor to repair portions of a copy protected diskette. The attempt could prevent further use of the diskette and its information. You will have to ensure that you have full read/write access to the files before they go bad to be able to make repairs when they become necessary. The possibility of needing to make those repairs will be reduced if you are diligent in making backups and in keeping your hard disk and diskettes in excellent condition, both physically and electronically.

You should correct problems with your applications by deleting the bad file and recopying it from a good backup or the original distribution diskette. The data you generate and the text files you create also should be repaired this way. Only in cases of crashes during a session where it is worth your time and frustration to attempt to recover the data should have to get down to the track and sector level to make repairs. The more valuable the data being generated, the more sensitive you should be to the need for keeping it backed up.

On networked systems and those with hard disks, the backup of critical data can mean making an additional copy of the files onto a diskette. Once the processing is complete, the final file can be placed in the proper storage location, and a single backup copy in a separate location. Be sure that both copies are properly labeled. Be sure also that the interim backup copies are eliminated for security reasons and to prevent anyone from attempting to use incomplete or incorrect data when it comes time to process that information again.

Partition

The reasons a large hard disk should be divided into smaller logical disks are almost as numerous as the megabytes on the disk itself. Backing up a smaller disk is easier. Using tape backup system and a compression feature, between 20Mb and 160Mb can be stored on a single tape. If the disk is larger than about 40Mb, you will benefit from partitioning your hard disk.

The hard disk used for Fig. 3-20 is not large, so the values you see here are smaller than should be expected when partitioning a large hard disk. The screen indicates that there is only about 5Mb of free space on this disk. Any partition to be made must be smaller than the available free space.

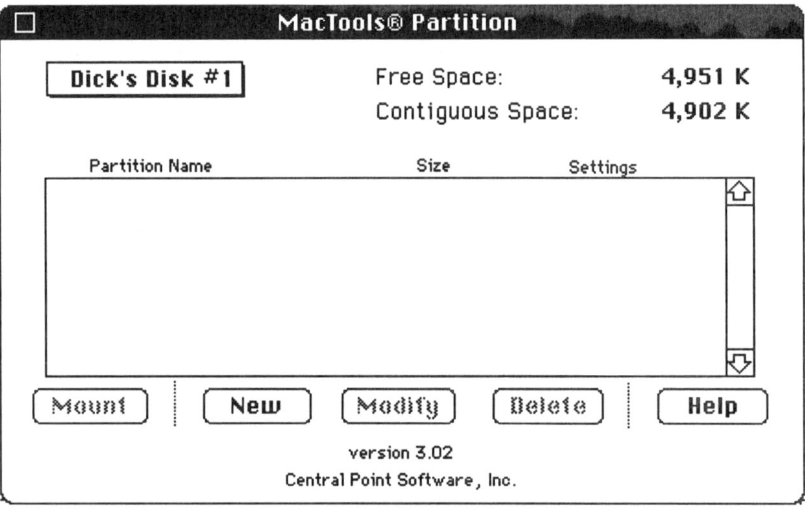

3-20 MacTools Partition opening screen

In Fig. 3-21, 1Mb partition has been made in the available free space. It is titled "Part #2." You have a lot of flexibility when you name your partitions. Partition names that indicate the contents of the partition are most useful. Names, such as "programs," "AutoCAD," "Cadkey," etc., can be helpful, especially if your system is used by more than one person. My word processor folder has separate folders for each of my children. Soon, I'm either going to have to set up a multi-station net or put a lock on the door. All things considered, I'd better start saving for a network and a few more stations.

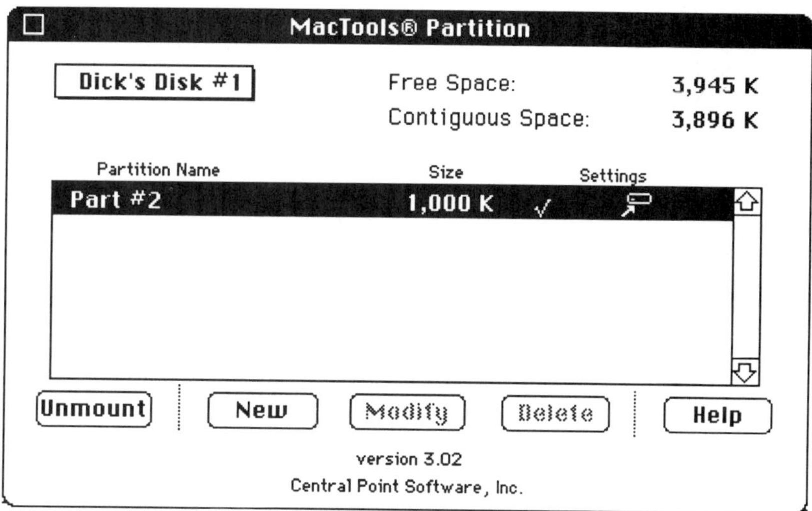

3-21 MacTools Partition screen with a partition installed

Each of the divisions made by Partition will appear to your system like a separate physical drive. With the exception of your startup drive, they will all be equal in features and limitations. You will have to do a little planning before you start using Partition and before you start loading files onto the various drives.

Segregating by function is a good way to keep things easy to find. I have one system with enough storage capacity that it makes sense to have multiple drives. The startup drive holds all of the necessary files for getting the system online. A CADD package and its folders are on another drive, and a word processor and its folders are on another. The small drive that remains holds various utility programs, and one section is reserved for new software testing.

This division of responsibility allows you to get things done faster in the individual areas. The drawings files are on the same drive with the CADD package, so the system doesn't have to look too far to find any of them. Partitioning also simplifies backing up a single folder at the end of the day or week.

Part 2
Fifth Generation Software

4
CHAPTER

DiskLock

Version: 2.0.1
System requirement: Macintosh Plus, SE, SE/030, II, IIx, IIcx
Compatibility: Any SCSI hard disk.
      May be used with AppleShare but not
        recommended for fileservers.
      Will FolderLock only on non-SCSI hard disks
      Will not work on Bernoulli disks.
      Will FolderLock floppies.

DiskLock is a security utility for the files on your storage media. Its purpose is to password-protect your programs and data files. Depending on your needs, you can bury your system's software in so much protection that it will be time to quit before you are able to launch the first application. How much protection is enough and how much is too much will be determined by your need to keep your information confidential and your need to be able to access it and perform necessary tasks.

A good security system will have more than one level of protection for the items being protected. The room, office, or building where the computer is physically located should have lockable doors and might even justify an alarm system of some description. The data in the computer should not be unique; you have backup copies of the information kept off-site. There were people who have said that the only real purpose for any lock is to ensure that an honest person remains honest. If someone insists on getting into your computer and viewing or copying your files assume that they can do it.

Before breaking the seal on the envelope containing the DiskLock diskette, think about passwords. You are going to need at least one, and a few more wouldn't be a bad idea. If one password gets compromised, you will have another one ready immediately. Although there aren't too many rules concerning what should be used as a password, there are many rules for what *not* to use as a password. DiskLock will accept a password that is 1 to 26 characters in length. An 8-character password usually is complex enough that the casual hacker isn't going to break it; however, having several hundred characters in a password will not stop a determined thief. Remember that potential data thieves have access to computers and can write programs to be used for password breaking. It's been done before, and it will continue to happen.

Some things that should not be used as passwords are nicknames for you or any member of your family, birth dates for you or any member of your family, anniversaries, names or nicknames of co-workers, or the company name or a company product name. You can use all of the letters of the alphabet, the numerals 0 through 9, and most of the special characters that are on the keyboard. The usable characters are:

! @ # $ % ^ & * ( ) − __ = + [ ] { } ; : ' " , . < > / ? \ ¦ ` and ~ .

Do not use the numeric keypad to type in any of these characters. The Option and Command keys also can be used; however, the Escape, Tab and Control keys can not be used. Be very careful about using spaces in a password. They can be confusing and can make breaking the password easier. To add to the number of possibilities, the passwords in DiskLock are case-sensitive.

The password, z1x4c7v9, might look complicated until you check the key positions. Then it becomes relatively easy to remember. I don't recommend this password because it is so simple. I also caution against leaving the piece of paper with your selected password anywhere where someone else can find it. If you must write it down, carry the paper with you at all times. Try to generate passwords that you can memorize, so it isn't necessary for you to carry a written copy of it for any extended period of time. The longer it remains written down, the better the chance of compromise. Once your password is compromised, it will have to be changed. Now, you will have to memorize a new password. It would be better to protect your old password until changing it becomes necessary.

I mention the necessity of changing passwords for a reason: the longer a password is in a system, the greater the possibility that it will be compromised in some way. If the information in the system is valuable enough to warrant password protection, then it also is worth the time and effort to make periodic (but not regular) changes to the password that is protecting it. Government security regulations require that passwords be changed at regular intervals. The exact length of the interval usually depends on the nature of the information being protected. The more sensitive the data, the more often the password changes.

Unless your business is regulated by the same rules you can be more flexible with your changes. As long as you don't forget to make the changes, this flexibility can add a factor of safety to your protection scheme. Because only you know when you are going to change a password, anyone else will have more difficulty determining when you have changed your password. Changing your password at irregular intervals also will tend to expose any undetected compromises that have occurred since the last change.

The only real problem with passwords is that as soon as more than one person knows what the password is the security is lost. Even giving each person his or her own password has its limitations. The whole concept of security depends on cooperation and a sense of responsibility from everyone involved. I'm not sure which is harder to obtain; both present major difficulties.

Beyond the security aspects of having files protected with a password, DiskLock has other features that make it a useful utility. One feature that appeals to me is the ability to have the system locked while I'm away from it for whatever reason. For example, I leave my system to get a cup of coffee and, while I'm doing that, my 18-month-old grandson decides to demonstrate his computer illiteracy with great glee. Having my system locked at such times has definite advantages.

The business environment usually is a little safer. Accidents, however, still happen, and safety without shutdown is nice. Co-workers feel guilty when they cause data loss problems. Those that don't usually are ex-employees before they can create enough problems to warrant more serious action. I tend to think in unfavorable terms about people who think that the computer is there strictly for their entertainment.

DiskLock keeps a log of every lock and unlock, as well as every attempt to access the system while it is locked. This log can be helpful for training employees whose workstations are within reach of the public. Such measures might seem a bit more than is necessary for single users in the home. Occasionally, however, incidents do occur that require just this degree of protection and record keeping.

I also must comment on the fact that you cannot read the log without launching another program, which isn't a big problem but does make things a bit more complex than might be necessary. You also need to launch another program when you want to change the password. In some cases, this additional step might be an advantage rather than a problem. This arrangement adds limited amount of security. The user at the keyboard might not know where to find the necessary program, and booting from a floppy will not bypass the password requirement. After you start the system, you can be sure that it will remain secure even while you are away. The system will even do background tasks while in the locked state.

Letting your computer work while you are away from the keyboard is one of the many advantages of automation. You can go to lunch and relax, knowing that when you return that a spreadsheet or other activity will be complete. If you had to sit there and wait for the results, you would have to find something else to do.

Among the other features of DiskLock is a virus detector. This detector might be your first warning that you have been infected. The detector in DiskLock, however, is for DiskLock only. To get your hard disk cleaned up, you will need to purchase a virus protector/detector/killer program. Several are mentioned in this book.

5
CHAPTER

Fastback II

Version: 2.50
System requirement: 4.2 or higher
Compatibility: 512e or newer

Throughout this book, I've been telling you that you must backup your files. What I haven't been telling you is how to perform this function. Fastback II (Fig. 5-1) is one of the better known ways to make backup copies of your files. With this utility, you can make various types of backups.

In a way, there is an art to making backup copies of files. If you plan what you want to do and then follow that plan, you can have a current set of backups without having a fortune tied up in diskettes or tapes. Depending on the volume of work you do with your system, your tape and diskette needs will vary from only a few to as many as 100. The more data passing through the system and the larger the hard disks, the more media required to make

5-1   Fastback II's opening screen

the necessary backup copies. Fastback II's compression capability will provide some assistance. Compressing files saves space but will make the backup process a little slower. You will have to experiment with your system and your data to determine which is more valuable, the time or the diskettes.

Before you had Fastback II, you made backups by copying your files to diskettes. This process is reasonably sure but very slow. It also requires that you use more diskettes, because you cannot divide a file across two diskettes. With Fastback II, you will not have many of the problems you have learned to live with in the past. Now, with a program of regular backups, you will be able to perform this function in a minimal amount of time and with fewer problems. This operation benefits from planning ahead.

The first backup should be a complete backup of your system. Fastback II makes this process easy. The backup options menu (Fig. 5-2) shows you what will happen when you start backing up. What you see here is not all of the options that are available. Each of the boxes has a number of other options that will be displayed when you click on that box. When you release the mouse button, that option will be displayed. Working your way down the menu will allow you to customize Fastback II to meet your needs.

5-2 Fastback's Backup options

You also might want to make two copies of this backup. One copy can remain nearby, while the other copy should be placed in storage away from the computer. A different geographical location is best. This backup is sometimes known as the "fire file." Should the worst happen and you have to restore your files to a new system, this is the file you would use. Once you have this complete backup, you can begin working with smaller backups. The only files that will require backing up will be those that have changed since your last full backup. Under normal circumstances, only our data files and correspondence will need to be backed up.

All of your application and utility files are on the first backup. Under ideal conditions, you should make an incremental backup every evening before you shut the system off for the night. This daily backup will ensure that all of your work from that day is recorded both on your hard disk and on the backup media. Depending on policy, security requirements, and any number of other factors, this backup can be kept in the same location as the computer or you might want to store it off-site. When you return in the morning, you will be able to start right where you left off. If you are not required to retain these daily backups, you can reuse the diskettes to make the next backup.

At some point, you should update the first set of backup files that you made. Updating these backup files might be a matter of policy or personal preference. Off-site files should never be allowed to get more than three months out of date. Trying to rebuild more than one quarter's work can be very time-consuming. If your plan calls for updating the off-site backup quarterly, then you should have a set of partial backups that covers all of the changes during the intervening time. This plan might not be as practical as some. Keeping track of the incremental backup diskettes for a three month period might be a problem.

Performing incremental backups on a weekly basis might be easier because there will be fewer incremental diskettes to locate. Friday would seem to be the most logical day to do the weekly backup, so weekend disasters don't start your week out on the wrong foot. No one, however, likes to stay late on Friday just to be sure the system is backed up. Maybe Monday would be a better day to do the weekly. You then can give yourself a little time to finish your coffee and open your eyes while the computer is busy. Just be sure that you make a daily backup before leaving on Friday. I keep saying that Murphy's Law is valid because it is.

The other half of backing up is restoring. When something happens and you can no longer access your data, your backup copies become your prime source for the lost data. You now will find out just how careful you have been and how well you have followed your plan. You must use Fastback II (Fig. 5-3) to restore your files if they have been backed up with Fastback II because Fastback II uses a proprietary method for writing your data to the backup diskettes. No other program can read your files and copy

Restore Options

Confirmation Dialog: Off
Overwrite: Older Files Only
Icon Positions: Original Position
Create Empty Folders: No
Backup Date: Don't Change
Destination Folder: Original Folders

Need Help?
Click the mouse button on any menu to get help.

Reset Settings

5-3 Fastback II's Restore options

them onto your hard disk in ready-to-run form. In addition, the new version of Fastback II is not compatible with the older Fastback for the Mac. There also might come a time when a newer version of Fastback II will not be compatible with your current version.

You then will have to update all of your backup diskettes by restoring them to a hard disk using the old version and then backing them up again using the new version. A word of caution: establish an empty volume to do this type of updating. You also might have to lock all of your current files so that they are not changed as you restore these old files to a disk for the purpose of updating the backup file format.

This type of incompatibility is not unique with Fastback II. At one time or another, every piece of useful software I have ever found became obsolete when the new version was released. Whenever possible, the developer tries to provide a migration path into the new software. At times, this transition isn't possible. When that happens, you must make a decision. Do you stay with the software you have, which will not be supported forever, or do you move up to the latest version of the software and update all of your files?

This type of decision making isn't easy and it isn't cheap. Upgrading means both the cost of the new software and the time to change all of the files. Staying with the orphan version means that there might come a time when the product is no longer supported and your copies give up the ghost. The expenses involved then will be greater and the recovery will need much more pressing. You can use an "every other one" philosophy when upgrading software. You can buy version 1.0 and then wait until version 3.0 is released to upgrade everything. There are good arguments for and against this type of thinking.

Upgrading software with no better justification than that it's the latest is poor judgment and an expensive way to operate. Every time you upgrade, there is a period of learning involved. If the software is upgraded on a 12 to 15-month cycle, (typical for some developers), you will be repeating the learning phase for new software just about the time everybody has gotten comfortable with using the current version. Another consideration in upgrading is the developer's history. If the first copies out the door tend to have a few rough spots, you might want to delay long enough for the first users to find all of the problems and then get the developer's .02 or .03 version.

As a beta tester, I know that I try to find problems, as do the other testers. I also know that, no matter how hard I try, something will go undiscovered until there are a few thousand copies of the software on the street. I also know there are going to be users who will never read the manual and users who will find ways to make the program do things it was never designed to do.

The Instant menu (Fig. 5-4) is designed for those of you who aren't interested in doing anything more than making a full backup. The boxes near the bottom tilted Short Menus and Full Menus are for the folks who are going to take a little more time setting things up. Some users will derive more benefit from using more of the features in Fastback II.

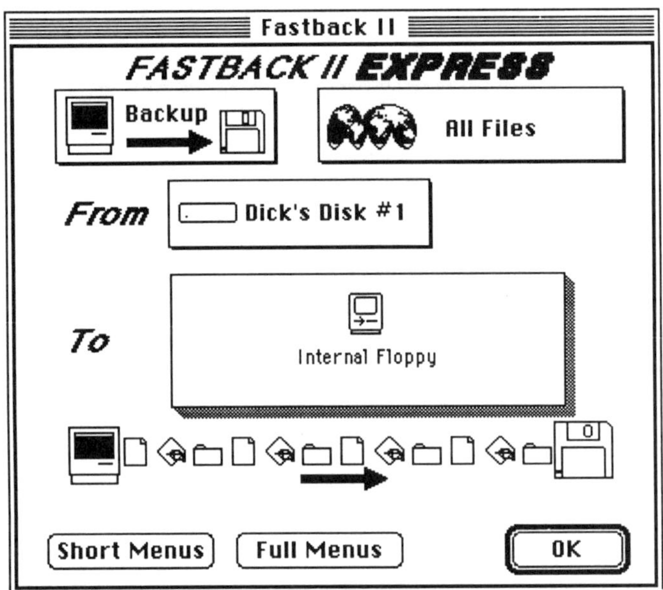

5-4 The Instant menu

You should not use the Instart menu for every backup that you make. You can make a full backup every time you back up; however, a full backup takes much longer than some of the other options. If time is no problem, then perhaps doing a full backup of your system on a daily or weekly basis is the way you want to go. If you do a full backup once a week, then you are subject to losing the information generated during the week, unless you do a lesser backup each day.

There are two types of partial backups: a differential backup and an incremental backup. They have some significant differences. An incremental backup appends the changed files to the end of the last full backup. It also marks the files it appends, so when you do the next incremental backup, it will not back up any files that have not changed since the last incremental backup. You can rebuild all of your files from the last full backup to the last incremental backup, with the differences between the backups preserved. If these variations are important, then the incremental backup should be your choice. To restore all your files to their current state, you will need your last full backup plus all of the diskettes that you have used for incremental backups.

If you do not need to preserve the intermediate changes, then a differential backup is indicated. This type of backup makes backup copies of all the files changed since the last full backup. The differential backup does not mark the copied files for reference. When the next differential backup is made, all of the files changed since the last full backup will be copied. You need only the full backup diskettes and the last differential backup to restore all of your files.

Which method or combination of methods you choose to use for backing up your data is immaterial. The important point is that you have made a choice and are making regular backups. I prefer to use the full and differential methods. This combination allows me to put the full backup diskettes away until they are needed and keep only the few diskettes necessary for making a differential backup. I have not found it necessary to preserve the intermediate versions of my files. If that becomes necessary, I will have to change my way of doing things. Be sure to make special labels for or mark the stock labels on the disks you use for backup diskette identification. There might be a more frightening event than to see your backup diskette being reinitialized, but I can't think of one right now. Diskette initialization, or formatting, erases all the information that was on the media.

Before you consider your backup complete, you should have a set of labels to identify the diskettes. Figure 5-5 shows one way that Fastback II makes your housekeeping easier. You need to have a sheet or roll of labels on-hand. They should be one of the

Print Labels

Paper Is: ○ One Label Wide
         ● Three Labels Wide

Labels To Print: 3

☒ Number Volumes   Start With Number: 1

Volume Name:

Date: 1/17/91

Format: 800K Double-Sided Floppy

[Cancel]   [OK]

5-5 The Print Label menu

first things you purchase after you buy enough blank diskettes to hold at least a few full backups. Practicing safe hex isn't something you can do from time to time; it must be a way of life when dealing with your computer. How many labels you need to print will depend on how much data you are going to backup and whether or not you are going to allow Fastback II to compress the data as it makes the backup copy.

The advantage of data compression is that it takes up less diskette space. The disadvantage is that it takes longer to make the backup copy. You will have to determine which you have more of, time or diskettes. Either way, you will have to take the time to back up. For full backups of large hard disks, the savings in diskettes can be worth considering.

One of the better uses for compressed backup files is archival storage. Archiving is used when you don't really need the file immediately accessible on your hard disk, but you also don't want to put it into the Trash Can. Using Fastback II to make a compressed backup copy of a file is a way to preserve the file without wasting hard disk space. Whenever you need the file again you can restore the file to the hard disk. Because every file you want to preserve will not require a separate diskette, you can store these archives together on a specially marked diskette.

The old adage, GIGO, is still true. When garbage goes in, garbage will come out. Even if you are positive that you haven't put any garbage into your system, you must continuously maintain it to insure that none comes out.

Fastback II also provides you with the ability to use tape, rather than diskettes, for your backup copies. You will have only a relatively small cartridge rather than a stack of diskettes to maintain. There is a cost difference, just like there is a capacity difference. Again, you will have to weigh the factors for and against going to a tape backup system. A 20Mb tape and 25 800 K diskettes will store about the same amount of information without compression. The number of diskettes drops to about 20 with the advent of the new 1.44Mb drives. The tapes and drive will be used only for backups. They can not become part of your system's mass storage capability. An external diskette drive can be used both for backups and for storage of information that is to be accessed while operating.

For backing up networks or systems with large or multiple hard disks, tape usually is the best media choice. The only better possibility, which will be coming soon, is optical disks. With tape, there are usually two types of backup schemes. One type makes a bit-by-bit copy of the disks without regard to content. This type is a virtual, or mirror, copy of the disks. The other scheme is a file-oriented backup. This backup preserves the structure of the files as it copies them. It also will eliminate the fragmentation of the files as they are copied.

The advantage of using the mirror type of backup is that it can be done quickly. The disadvantages are that it is an all-or-nothing process and that it does not remove the fragments. The restored disks will have everything that was on them in exactly the same place and the same condition. The file-oriented tape procedure will be a bit slower, but it retains the structure and thereby allows you to do a partial restore of the backup file contents. The defragmentation of the files is an added benefit from using this procedure. Fastback II uses a file-oriented scheme for its tape backup utility.

One of the disadvantages of having a powerful backup utility program package like Fastback II is that there are so many settings to remember on so many different menus. It is very thoughtful of the developers to have provided for people like me. Fastback II has a setup feature that allows you to set everything properly for the type of backup you want to make. You then can save those settings to a file. The same can be done for different types of backups, as well as restores. By giving each of the files a descriptive filename, you can reduce the possibility of future errors. Your backup procedure then becomes a matter of selecting the proper setup file, making the backup copies, and properly storing the media.

Another feature available in Fastback II is called macros. A macro is a series of recorded keystrokes and mouse maneuvers that are played back to the computer to form a complex command. The way you do some tasks never varies; the keystroke sequence and mouse clicks are the same every time you invoke the routine, program, utility, etc. This type of unchanging sequence can be placed into a file, so you don't have to type it every time you want to use it. When you need to perform the activity again, you just call up the macro and your system will respond just as if you had done all the key pressing and clicking yourself. Two things will be different. First, the file won't make typos or mis-clicks. Second, the command will be entered much faster.

Don't worry about the file running too fast for your computer. Keyboarded input can be handled at the rate of about 1,500 words a minute. If your typing speed is greater than this rate, you might have to go to a different form of input. The instructions being read into your system by a file can come at a more rapid rate. The microprocessor inside your computer is running at a speed of 8 megahertz or more; therefore, it can cope with a few million bits of information every second. (Note the change in time measurement.)

6
CHAPTER

Suitcase II

Version: 1.2.6
System requirement: 4.1 or higher, Font/DA Mover 3.8 or
higher.
Compatibility: Any Macintosh 512KE, Plus, SE, or II.

There are already suitcases in your system. Why would you need another suitcase? Suitcase II (Fig. 6-1) isn't just another suitcase to clutter up your electronic landscape. Suitcase II is more like a suitcase organizer than just a suitcase. Perhaps a better way to describe this utility would be that it is a resources manager. These resources are things like program code, desk accessories, typeface shape files, dialog box layout files, menu content, and format files.

Suitcase II contains some resources that you will want to have readily available at all times when your system is running. There are others that you will need only when you are performing certain types of tasks. Some users will want to have more than

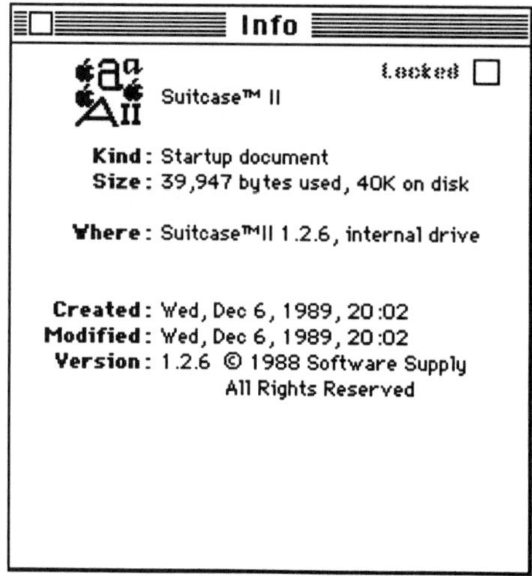

6-1 Suitcase II's Get Info screen

the 15 desk accessories (DAs) and 500 fonts allowed by the operating system limits. Even if you are not trying to exceed these limits, the power and flexibility of Suitcase II can provide you with a number of advantages.

If you have total control over the number and type of files that are open within the System Folder under all conditions, you can improve your system's performance. You might not need to have every font of every typeface on your hard disk available while you are doing a simple file transfer to a local bulletin board. You also might want access to some of these resources from within applications that normally don't allow such access. Suitcase II provides you with the flexible control you need to make your use of your system as efficient as you know how to make it.

To determine how big your System File has gotten, look at its Get Info screen. Compare that screen with the Get Info screen for the System File on your Apple distribution diskettes. You might be surprised. You should be able to copy the System File to a diskette. If it gets too big, you will not be able to make new startup diskettes. Even if it isn't too big to fit on a diskette, you need enough room on the same diskette to copy the other information you wanted.

The System File illustrated in Fig. 6-2 is from my hard disk with only a few things added. The bare-bones System File is only about 265K, while a fully-loaded System File can exceed 1Mb.

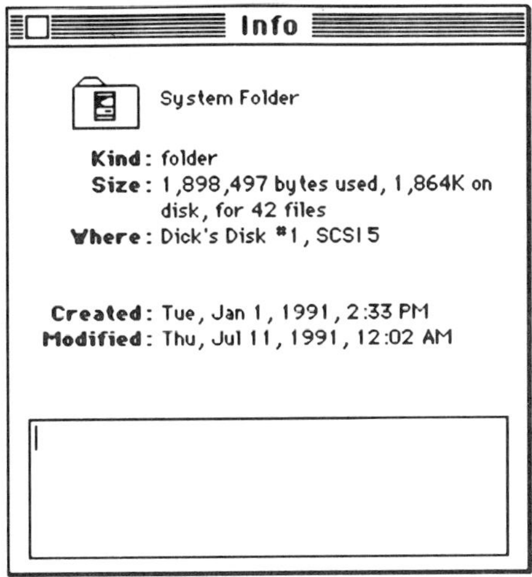

6-2 A System File Get Info screen

Obviously, the fully-loaded file will not fit on a floppy. You should have a copy of the bare-bones version handy to use when you are trying to generate new startup diskettes.

After Suitcase II is properly installed, it is accessed via the Apple menu. As shown in Fig. 6-3, Suitcase II will appear above the standard Apple utilities. You can access the menu in every application.

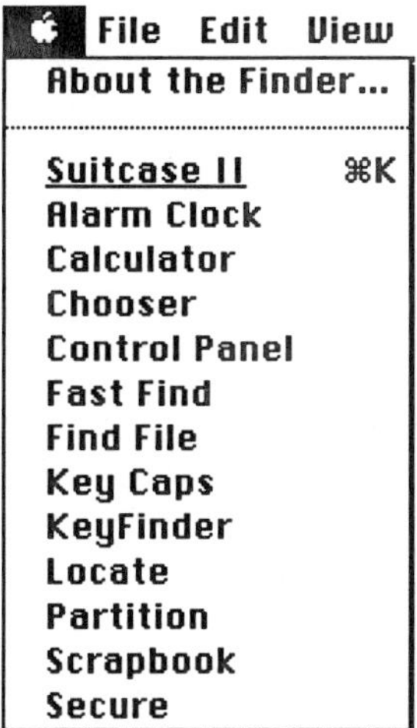

6-3 The Apple Menu with Suitcase II

Once you get all your Suitcase II files organized, you might want to use the services of the Font & Sound Valet. This utility program, provided with Suitcase II, compresses the contents of your suitcases. The files will be decompressed as they are read into RAM, so you will not experience any difficulty. In a few cases, you might notice that it takes just a little longer for the files to be loaded, assuming that you are watching very carefully and using a stopwatch to measure these little differences. The suitcases on your hard disk will remain compressed until you decompress the suitcase with the Font & Sound Valet again. I don't think that you will want to trade the hard disk space for the speed increases in most, if not all, cases. The time losses occur only when you are loading a suitcase. The space loss is a permanent thing.

The utilities illustrated in Fig. 6-4 are the default Apple utilities. There will be additional listings if you have other DAs installed. The same is true of the listings displayed when you click on any of the remaining radio buttons. Suitcase II sorts the displays for you, so you aren't trying to deal with everything in a single list, making your work a bit easier.

6-4 Suitcase II's opening screen

A bit farther down the screen there is a Settings selection. These settings (Fig. 6-5) are the beginnings of your configuration, or customization, of Suitcase II. How far you go or whether you go at all is your choice. You don't have to live with the defaults, and you don't have to live with your own modifications. Both are subject to change at your command.

☒ **Show icon at startup**

⌘**-key for Suitcase II DA:** `K`

In ⬤ menus, place the Suitcase II DA:
○ **At top of DAs**　　◉ **Alphabetically**

Font and ⬤ menus modifier key is:
◉ **Option**　　○ ⌘　　○ **Shift**

Font menus show font names in their own typefaces when modifier is:
◉ **Pressed**　　　　○ **Not pressed**

Shorten ⬤ menu when modifier is:
◉ **Pressed**　　　　○ **Not pressed**

[**"Power User" Settings...**]

[**OK**]　　　　　[**Cancel ⌘.**]

6-5　The first settings screen

The Power User screen (Fig. 6-6) might or might not be correctly titled. The first selection probably should be checked for all users. Pulling down a font menu to find that what you want isn't available can be frustrating. The reverse is just as true. It might be more frustrating when you have just finished opening a suitcase for the sole purpose of using some of the fonts that it contains.

Modifying the second selection will depend on how you are using your system. Being able to open 12 suitcase files can be more than enough for many users. The contents of each suitcase will be more the determining factor. If you can keep the number of open suitcases low, your RAM management will improve. The more files you allow to be open, the more RAM space you will

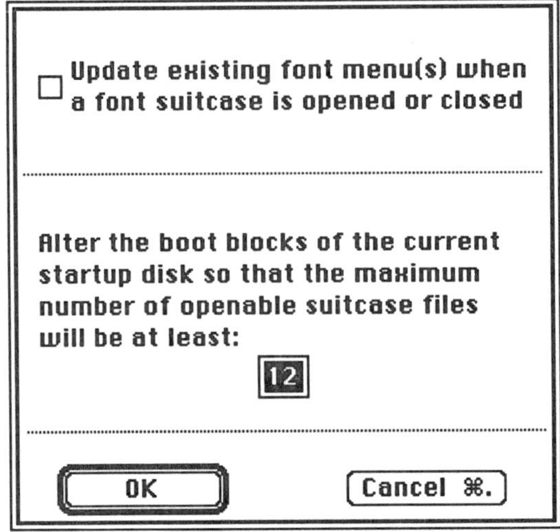

6-6 The Power User settings screen

require. Your RAM is limited. The space reserved by the boot blocks is not available for applications. (I prefer to keep the maximum available for applications.)

Suitcase II will make as many specialized suitcases as you have space to store. You can have an application specific suitcase for each program you use. If you do generate your suitcases this way, you will be duplicating some of your font files, which might or might not be a problem. Duplications mean increased space consummation with no increase in function. Users with small hard disks (80Mb or less) might want to look at developing suitcases along more generic lines, possibly eliminating file duplication. If that isn't possible, then you should try to minimize the number and size of the files that must be duplicated.

The Font Harmony utility (Fig. 6-7) provides a number of useful services. It will renumber font files when there are conflicts. All the font files will have unique names, which is important if you tend to move files from folder to folder. Like every other computer, the Macintosh doesn't like to have two files with the same name in the same place at the same time. The computer tends to get confused when you start calling for the filename that is duplicated. Confused computers crash. Those that don't crash tend to make hash of both files, which could be worse. There is a limited amount of logic available to the computer when selecting

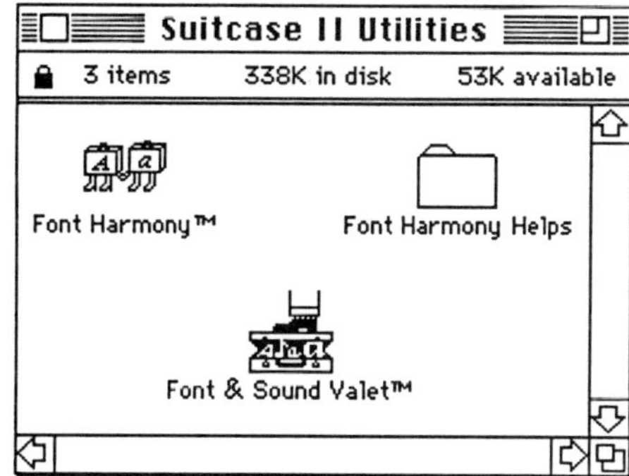

6-7 The Font Harmony utilities

files that have the same name but reside in different locations. The logic prevents some problems but not all of them. The safest course of action is to eliminate filename duplications.

Font Harmony also will merge all of the fonts of a specific typeface into a single family. This grouping should make it easier for you to select the font you want to use in a specific place. It also should make it easier for you to select the fonts you want to be available for various applications. 8-point type isn't too handy when you are trying to build banners. Neither is 144-point type too useful when you're writing contracts. Both fonts have their uses and both can remain on your hard disk at all times. Having Suitcase II suitcases on floppy diskettes for special purposes is another possibility.

Fonts that are used on rare occasions might be placed in a suitcase on a floppy diskette. The hard disk space will be freed while still allowing you to have the font files immediately available. Just remember the capacity of your diskettes when you start filling that suitcase. After compression, the suitcase must fit on a single diskette or it will have to remain on the hard disk. Those of you with the new 1.44Mb drives will enjoy the increased space available to you. Just remember that they too have limits and you cannot stuff more than their capacity onto them.

Part 3
Magic Software, Inc.

7
CHAPTER

AutoSave II

Version: 1.11
System requirement: 4.2 or higher
Compatibility: Any Macintosh

AutoSave II is a neat little utility program that can be the lifeline you need when everything goes wrong. Properly installed, AutoSave II writes your current work to disk at regular intervals.

I don't know how many of you have been hard at work for an extended period of time only to have the screen go blank. Writers working on a deadline, among others, will appreciate the blink of the drive light as AutoSave II does its thing and writes away. Most programs don't save your work until you exit the program or initiate some other action.

Installed into the System Folder, AutoSave II is ready to go to work immediately. You might want to review the default settings on the Control Panel menu (Fig. 7-1) before charging off to solve the world's problems before lunch.

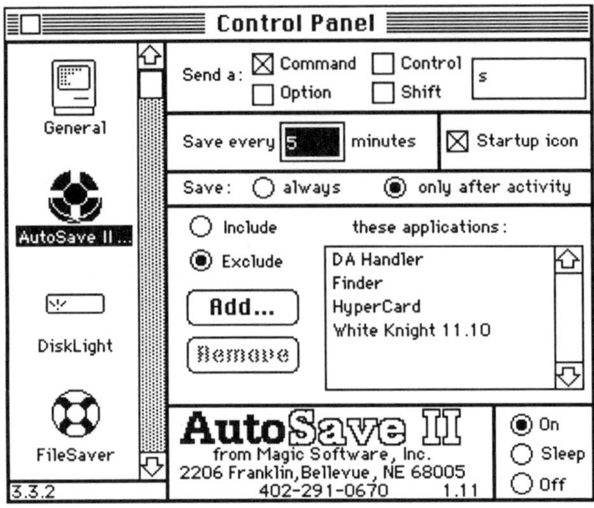

7-1   AutoSave II Control Panel

The first item on the menu is the command to be used to start an AutoSave II save operation. Select a keypress combination that isn't being used by another program. Next, you'll want to set the time interval for the save operation. Word processor files save rather quickly. Unless you're not a fast typist the save will be almost transparent. The time interval limits are from 1 to 99 minutes. Because security is a consideration, 5 minutes is a good starting point. You can adjust for longer or shorter intervals at any time by pulling down the option, or Apple, menu and selecting the proper control panel.

AutoSave II's lifesaver icon is almost unique. Note that the dark stripes are horizontal and vertical. Another utility discussed in this book has a similar icon with the stripes on the diagonal. You can check whether or not you want to see it every time you start your system. I like to see it so I have the option checked. It might be a false sense of security, but I know that under almost any circumstance everything I put into the system will be written to the disk.

Another option is when to save. You have two choices: always or only after activity. There is no need to save what's already saved or waste space attempting to save nothing. I've set my option to save after something's happened.

You also can select which things are to be saved. The next section of the Control Panel menu deals with which programs will start or not start the AutoSave II clock. By default, AutoSave II ignores activity by the DA Handler, Finder, and Hypercard. When any of these programs are running, they don't start the AutoSave II clock. Should you want to use AutoSave II with Hypercard, you can initiate a save manually by using the key-press combination you selected earlier. Which way you set Auto-Save II will depend on whether you have more applications you want to have AutoSaved or more that don't require AutoSaving. Regardless, be consistent and set the proper button and enter all of the program names.

There is one more small box in the lower right-hand corner of the menu. There are three buttons in the box. One of them is always selected. The default setting is On. If you know that you don't want AutoSave II active for a particular session, switch to the Sleep option. This setting will deactivate AutoSave II until you switch back to the On option or until the next time you start your system. The Off option means what it says. Turning Auto-Save II off is just like dumping it in the trash can except that it still occupies disk space. I feel this switch is unnecessary.

If you're going to have a utility like AutoSave II installed, then it should be launched and running every time the power is turned on. I use the Sleep switch because I haven't taken the time to add all of the programs that should be on the exceptions list. There also are times when you might be doing something that doesn't require saving. Communications, like using White Knight with it's own save feature, is one possibility.

There are some incompatible programs that AutoSave II can't save. They currently are:

MacPaint, v. 2.0
Microsoft Word v. 1.05
QuickKeys
Tempo II
Communications or terminal programs that use the
    Command-S or Control-S key combination

One of the first requirements for being able to recover information is that the information was stored someplace to begin with. When AutoSave II reaches its first time mark, it will present you with a window (Fig. 7-2) to verify what you want saved and where you want it stored. If you are in a session that does not

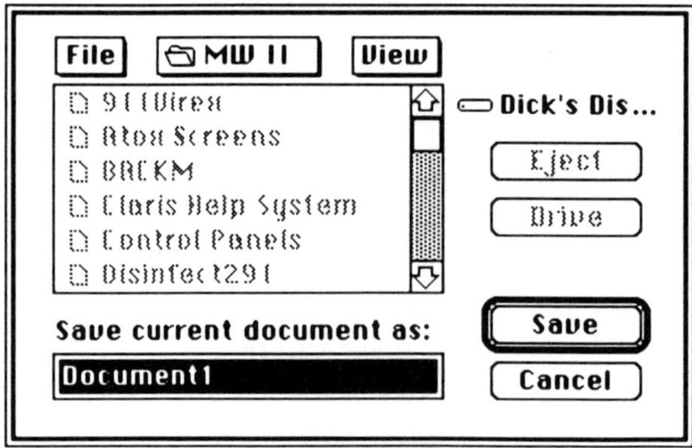

7-2 The first save

require AutoSaving, you can click on the Cancel option and put AutoSave II to sleep. Otherwise, take the actions necessary to establish a place for your work to be saved and let AutoSave II do its thing while you do yours.

If information was not stored, trying to recover it is useless. With AutoSave II quietly waiting in the background to save your files every few minutes, you should never be more than a few sentences away from having your file saved. Little, if any, of your work will be lost in the event that something not so nice happens.

8
CHAPTER

Backmatic

Version: 1.13
System requirement: 4.2 or higher
Compatibility: Any Macintosh

Backmatic (Fig. 8-1) is a backup program. Its purpose is to remind you to make another copy of your work. Backmatic is different from an imaging program in that it makes copies only of those files that have been changed since it was installed.

Making backup copies of the work you perform should be a mandatory part of your computing procedures. In a network environment, this process might be someone else's responsibility. Regardless of the policy, you still must be responsible for your own work. If something happens and the network backup fails, you still should be able to reload your work and continue.

Policies are good guides but should not be cast in stone that common sense and personal responsibility are excluded. Users of stand-alone systems must be sure that their work is backed up,

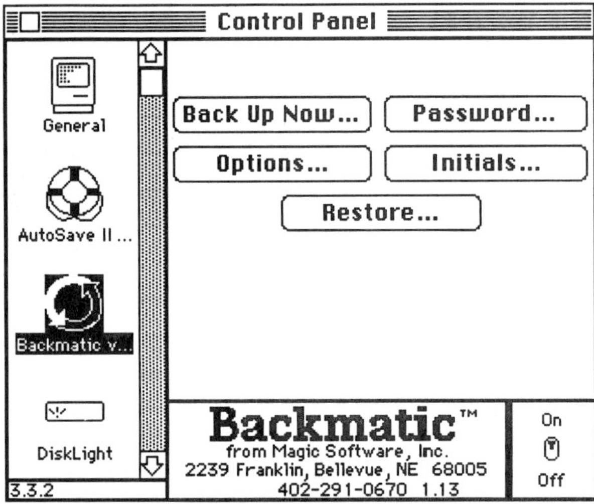

8-1   The Backmatic Control Panel

especially in situations where more than one person uses the system. Mistakes happen. Mechanical failures happen. There are power outages.

The best way to minimize the problems these incidents can cause is to prepare for them in advance, or prepare for the worst while hoping for the best. The most complimentary thing that can be said about a backup policy is that not even one byte has been lost since the policy was initiated. There are two possible reasons for the success of a backup policy. It might never have been tested or it might have been tested and passed with flying colors.

Backmatic for the individual or the network Macintosh user is a simple means of making backups at logical times. The "matic" in Backmatic implies some sort of automatic type of capability. The option menu (Fig. 8-2) should be your first clue as to just how automatic Backmatic can be. On the left side of the menu, you determine when you want to make backups. While on the right side, you determine what you want those backups to contain. Figure 8-3 shows the screen that is used to exclude or include specific files.

For most business users, a daily backup should be adequate. Home users might find a weekly backup sufficient. Waiting any longer is an invitation to disaster. For high volume or ultra-sensitive usage, more frequent backups might be warranted. Back-

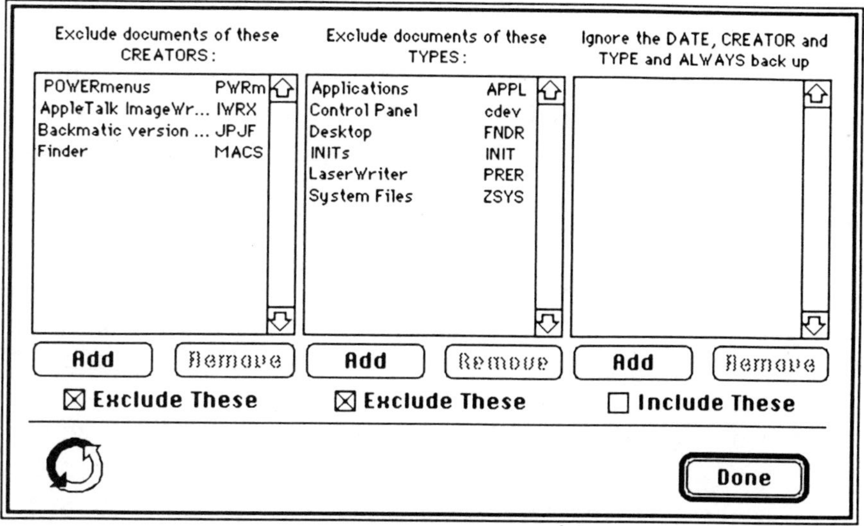

8-2 The Backmatic Options screen

8-3 Backmatic Document Selection screen

matic is flexible enough to cope with all of the above without breaking. How long it will take to perform a backup will depend on a number of factors: how much is there to be backed up, what type of media is being used to hold the backup files, how large the hard disk is that must be read to locate all of the files which require backup, and whether more than one hard disk is to be searched.

Determining what should be backed up and when is a critical consideration that must be answered in definitive terms for each independent user and each organization. Programs that are present on diskettes, which are copies of the originals received from the developers, need not be backed up. The file holding your customization or configuration of that application should be backed up every time you make a change to that file. There also should be a single backup of your basic system configuration.

If the worst were to happen and you lost your hard disk, how long would it take you to duplicate the information on a new piece of hardware? How much is your time worth that you will spend on the duplication process? Is there anything you can do to shorten the process? Does it make dollars and sense to implement the changes? Write down a date now when you will have all of the changes made. Why a date now? Because a goal without a deadline is only a dream, and dreaming doesn't make anything happen.

Now that you are making regular backups, how many of them do you need to keep? When Backmatic makes a new backup, it copies only the files that have been changed since the last backup. Some users will be able to keep a week of daily backups on a single diskette. Others will be able to place only a day's work on a diskette. Large databases and various types of graphic files might require more than one diskette. Backmatic is fully able to split a file across two or more diskettes. A full backup, or mirror, of your system hard disk should be made at regular intervals.

Business users should keep a full backup of each system or the file server in a secure location off-site. This location could be a safe deposit box at the bank or possibly a special safe at the corporate lawyer's office. There also are commercial services that will store your critical data for a fee. Taking a copy of the files home over the weekend is a good thought and an effective way to have at least one copy of everything away from the computers that use it. Those disks, however, it should not be the only copy available.

A full backup is a byte-by-byte copy of everything on the disk. Your daily or weekly backups should be saved until this mirror copy is updated. You also can make a full backup of your hard disk without recopying all of your software. Less time and fewer diskettes will be required to make a full backup if it is done this way. Using this method also reduces the possibility of unauthorized copies of your software becoming available to other users. You also can use Backmatic's password feature (Fig. 8-4) to help protect your data.

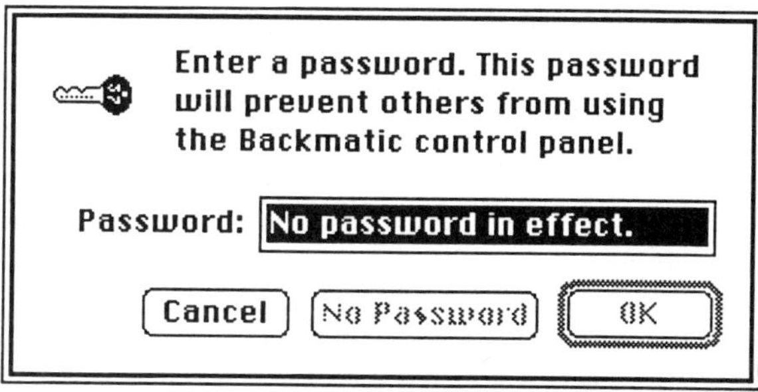

8-4 Backmatic's Password screen

Backmatic's options for scanning are such that you can be sure that every file that has been changed will be found; however, only those you have selected will be written into the backup folder. Remember that the drive must be mounted if Backmatic expects to scan it. The destination or target drive also must be ready to receive the information Backmatic is trying to save for you.

Portable users will find an additional feature in Backmatic that can prove useful. Backmatic monitors the battery power level and warns you at least once to perform a backup. There are a total of three alerts available; however, the first two are equipped with on/off switches that allow you to disable them. By the time the third alert is given, you should be doing your backup. Work done while battery power is low might not be saved to disk in a manner that allows it to be recovered with the charger active.

Having data backed up implies that there will be a time when it is necessary to restore that information to your system. Actually, it is not an implication; it is a fact. Hard drives do not last forever. In time, yours too will fail. A user begins to appreciate the need for backups usually at the time of the first failure. Every new user is told that backups are necessary and every new user hears tales of woe about work lost because it wasn't backed up. Every new user, however, must experience a loss of some magnitude before they understand that they must back up.

Backmatic's restore options (Fig. 8-5) range from a single selected file to all of the files that it has written. Backups can replace files still found on the hard disk, or they can be renamed and written to empty space, so both copies are available. Having an old copy and a new copy of some files can be useful when you are trying to determine what changes have been made to the file during the period between the copy dates.

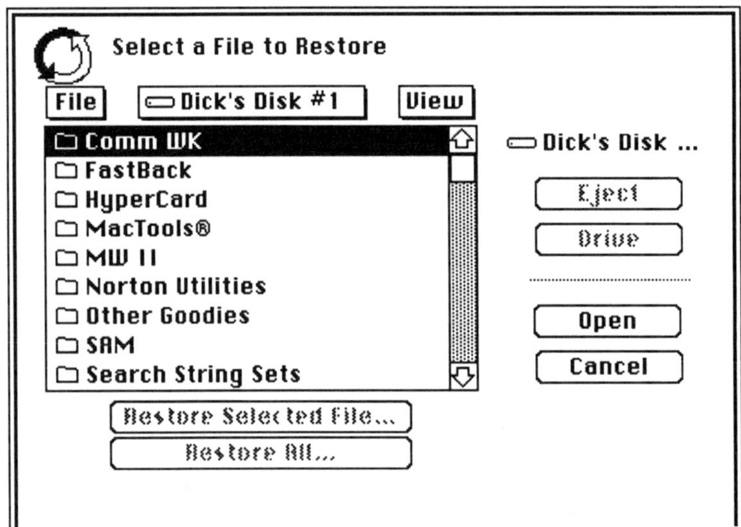

8-5 Backmatic's Restore screen

Backmatic's maintains logs of its backup activities (Fig. 8-6). It keeps one log that is specific to the backup folder in the backup folder and another log in the system folder. The system folder log is a master log. It contains information on all the files Backmatic has made copies of since it was installed. The information on each file should match. This information consists of the conditions and settings under which the copy was made. If there are

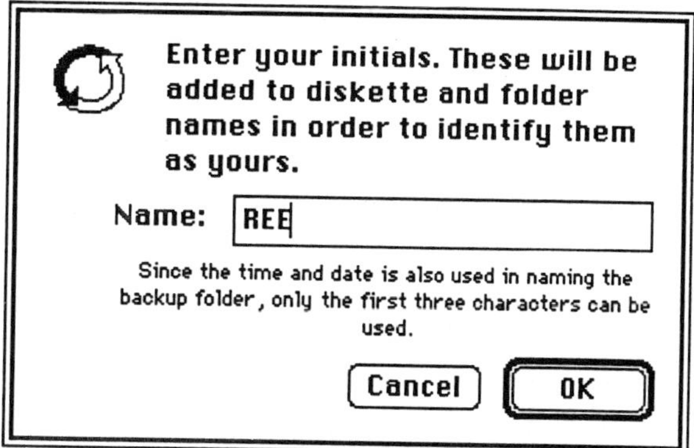

8-6 Backmatic's Initials screen

differences in the logs, any problems you might be experiencing could be coming from system problems, not Backmatic software problems.

9
CHAPTER

AntiToxin

Version: 1.4
System requirement: System 6.0 or higher for the application program. System 4.1 or higher for the INIT.
Compatibility: Macintosh Plus, SE, SE/030, II, IIx, IIcx

AntiToxin is a matched two-part protection package. The developer stresses that both the application and the INIT must be of the same version for AntiToxin to function properly. You can verify the version numbers of both programs by checking the Get Info screen on each program (Figs. 9-1 and 9-2), which is part of the File pull-down menu.

AntiToxin prevents the spread of an infection by locking the suspect file so that it cannot be launched. If the INIT is active, the application will not be able to open the file to attempt disinfection. To disinfect files, you must start your system with software

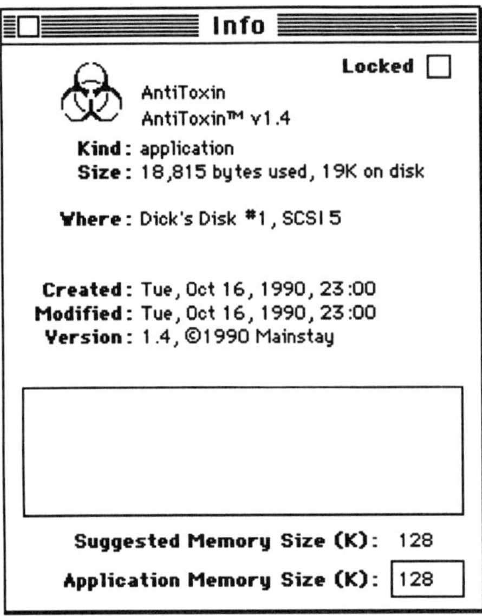

9-1 The Get Info screen for the INIT

9-2 The Get Info screen for the application

that does not have the AntiToxin INIT active in the system. This can be done by starting your system from a floppy diskette or by using a program, such as AAsk or INITpicker, to disable the AntiToxin INIT. Of the two, the developer recommends using the floppy diskette procedure.

To check your system for infection, you must first use the AntiToxin application program from the floppy diskette. Once this program is satisfied that there are no viruses present, you can install the INIT in your hard disk's system folder. You will need a backup copy of the AntiToxin diskette to make further checks of your hard disk.

The first thing to do after you have launched the AntiToxin application program is to tell it which disk it is to check. Figure 9-3 is an illustration of this screen. If you have only one hard disk mounted, then it's an easy choice. If you have more than one, sit back and relax with the manual while the program runs.

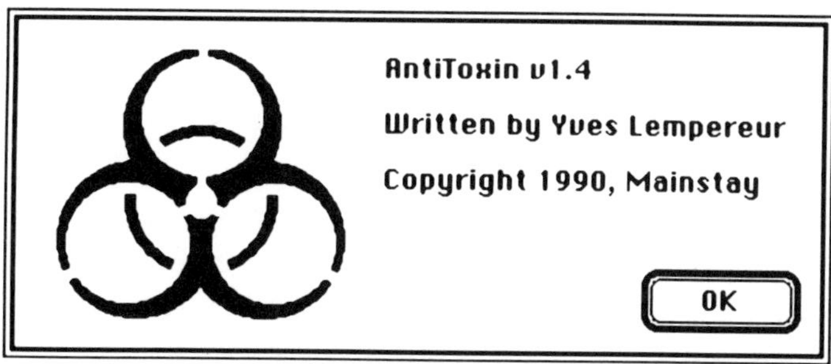

9-3 The AntiToxin opening screen

There are four counter windows displayed in Fig. 9-4. The first one keeps a running total of the files that have been checked. The second one reports the number of infected files discovered. Because this is a file number rather than an infection number, it will not indicate if there were any files that held more than one infection. The number of files repaired should equal the number of files found to be infected. Errors reported are the number of files that could not be checked for whatever reason. If you have booted from the floppy diskette, there should be very few, if any, errors reported. The last section displays the version number. The Checking line below the windows reports which file is currently being checked by AntiToxin.

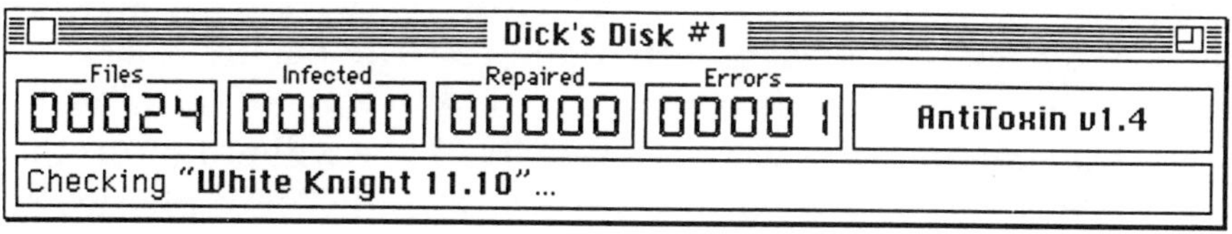

9-4 The Counter screen

If the number of files infected and the number of files repaired does not match at the end of the run, consider the job unfinished. There will never be more repairs than infections, but there can be less. Assuming that your hardware is operating properly, you'll need to run AntiToxin again. AntiToxin should be able to handle files that have been infected with more than one virus (a multiviral infection). I'm not sure whether or not I would be as well equipped. Because all of my software comes from known sources, a double-infected diskette would be very hard to cope with. Regardless of the source, including developers, I still check every disk before allowing it into my system.

Once you have your hard disk clean, it's time to check your diskettes. If you have two floppy drives, you can use one for AntiToxin and the other for checking. If you only have one drive, then use the AntiToxin application on your hard disk to check your floppies. After each diskette is processed, you will have a counter window on your screen. If you start another check before closing the open window, it will run properly as long as there aren't four tiled windows on display. AntiToxin will run up to four checks before you have to start closing windows. If you have only four diskettes to check, wait until after the last one to check out the various window contents. If you are going to check a large number of diskettes, I'd recommend that you close each window after you review the contents. This way you will never reach the limit of four windows and cause yourself further delay.

Be sure to unlock each floppy just before you insert it in the drive for checking. AntiToxin cannot check out the contents of a locked diskette. After it has been checked and repaired (if necessary), be sure to lock it again. You might have noticed that some developers have had the little shutter piece removed from their diskettes. Those diskettes are always locked and cannot be physically unlocked.

For those of you who know individuals who use DOS-based systems with those big floppy diskettes, you have a solution available. The write-protect stickers that come packaged with their diskettes will serve as a temporary write-enable mask for your diskettes. Do not leave these little black or silver tabs on your diskettes any longer than necessary. They will not harm the diskette or the label, but they will leave your diskettes physically unlocked.

Experience has proven that an unlocked diskette is an open invitation to trouble that seldom goes unanswered. Even a sole user in the privacy of his/her own home can find that these diskettes seem to breed problems. In an office or multiuser environment, unlocked diskettes are fair game for anybody's use. I agree that the tape across the window should cause them to wonder about using the diskette. Ever get in a hurry to get something backed up so you could get to another place without being late? Ever wonder where you got those diskettes when you go back to check on the files? This is sufficient reason to remove the tab immediately after checking the diskette.

Your software security measures should be much more than just ensuring that all of your file-laden diskettes are locked and that there are no active viruses in your system. How many other measures you need to take to ensure that your data remains secure will depend in part on the nature of the data. File integrity measures are the same for all users regardless of the data content. You need to do little things like reinitializing a diskette before placing new files on it. Remember my discussion about how file recovery programs work. Don't let the remains of your old files corrupt your new ones.

Storage of diskettes is also important, not only the location but also the environment. Store then in cool, dry, and dark places, away from as much electrical/electronic interference as possible. Keep them in containers that will limit the amount of dust and dirt that might get to them. Rotate them at regular intervals. The information written to floppy diskettes can fade over time. For business users, there should be at least one set of current backup diskettes off-site, in a secure location known and accessible to at least a few people.

The top shelf in one of your closets at home isn't my idea of a good off-site location. A bank safe deposit box, the company lawyer's office safe, a branch office safe, or a similar location is more appropriate. One idea that seems to work for a local company is a round-robin backup system. Every week, the company backs up its system to a tape at another office in a different city. It's all done via a modem and is automated so that it can be done during the late night hours of low rates and light traffic.

10
CHAPTER

Microcom 911 Utilities

Disk 1 contains only part of the 911 Utilities (Fig. 10-1). Note also that there is a System Folder on this diskette. This means that it is a boot diskette. Your system can be started from this diskette.

Disk 2 (Fig. 10-2) also has a System File included. The Virex antivirus program is covered in another chapter. The Complete Undelete utility (Fig. 10-3) is in the System Folder, along with the System and Finder Files.

The balance of the 911 utilities are in the Utilities Folder. Figure 10-4 shows the icons for those utilities.

Complete Undelete

There are two ways you can buy this utility. If you purchase the 911 Utilities, you will get Complete Undelete, Sector Collector,

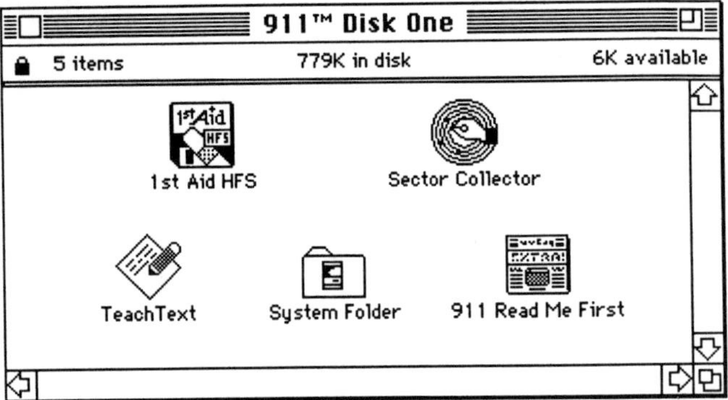

10-1 The Microcom disks (disk 1)

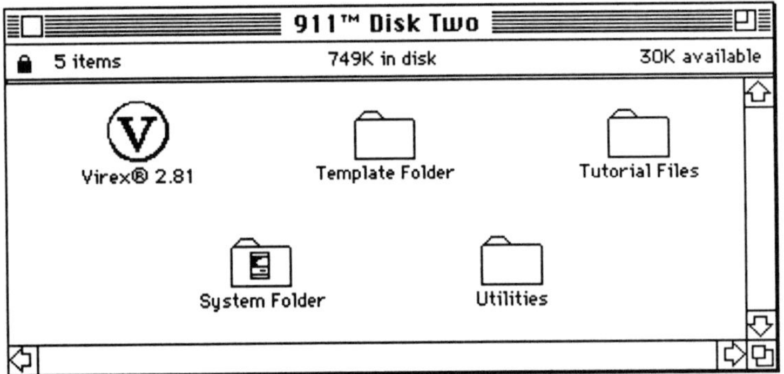

10-2 The Microcom disks (disk 2)

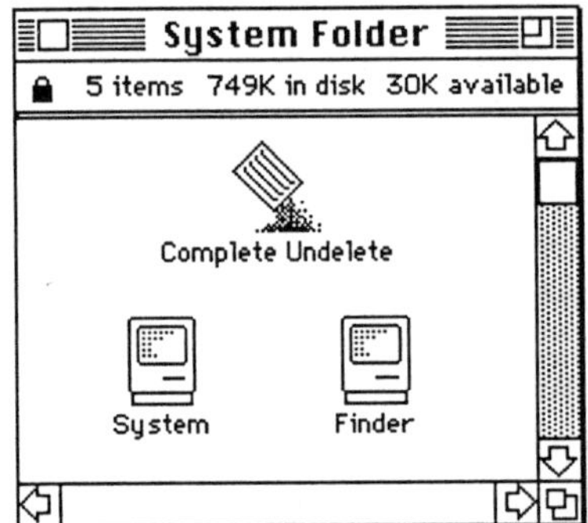

10-3 The System folder (disk 2)

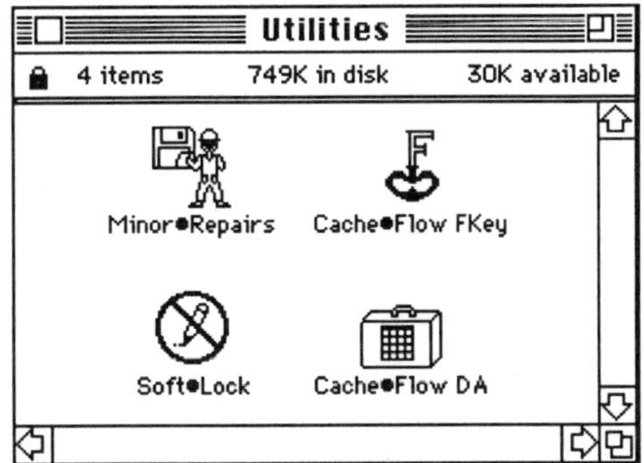

10-4 The Utilities folder (disk 2)

and Virex. You also can purchase Complete Undelete as a stand-alone utility. Virex also is sold as a stand-alone.

Complete Undelete is a utility that everyone who errs will appreciate. For those perfect users who never do anything wrong, reading this section might be a waste of time. This utility will help you recover things that have been trashed but that really should have been saved.

Like all good programs, this one has its limitations. They aren't really all that bad. Complete Undelete works by making a log of the files that are moved into the Trash Can. Files that were trashed before Complete Undelete was installed will not be recoverable using Complete Undelete. It still might be possible to recover these files; you just can't use Complete Undelete to do the job. Even after Complete Undelete has been properly installed and is maintaining its log, there still will be files that it cannot recover.

When you install this utility, you will specify the size of the log file. Until this log is full, there is a very good probability that you will be able to recover 100 percent of the file. As the log becomes full, the oldest files become unprotected. The system will be able to overwrite the sectors that contain the information this file is holding. As this happens, the information from the first file is gone forever. When the system overwrites a sector, it doesn't apply white-out and write on top of the clean surface. It gets right to the heart of the matter and magnetically changes the bits on the media. Once these changes are made, it is impossible to put them back in their former positions. They might return there if you were to write the same information into the same sectors again; just don't expect them to get back into alignment on their own.

Now that the things that can't be done are out of the way, just what can Complete Undelete do for you? As mentioned above, any file that is being protected by Complete Undelete that hasn't reached the end of the log should be recoverable. If it was protected but is no longer protected, it still is possible that some parts of the file can be recovered. Complete Undelete has two very nice features that make it easier to recover files that have lost their protection. The first one writes sectors of zeros. This will help keep the remaining information in its proper place. If the number of sectors lost isn't too great, the file still might be accessible, so you can rebuild the lost portions.

The technique used on text files is a bit different. Rather than fill your screen with pages of zeros, Complete Undelete will extract the recoverable text and write it into a new file that can then be opened with a word processor. Your rebuilding technique then is just retyping. This is not to imply that the retyping is going to be easy or that you won't have to spend a few hours work before everything is recovered.

Throughout, you might notice that undeleting isn't the easiest task to perform. One of the things that can make it a bit easier for any utility you choose to use is keeping your files as unfragmented as possible. (Another advantage of not having fragmented files is that your system will operate more efficiently.) Fragmentation is a natural occurrence and there isn't any good way to avoid it. The only thing you can do is use an optimizer utility, which will eliminate fragmentation. If this is done on a regular basis, it doesn't take long and goes a long way toward making recovery operations as painless as possible.

Warning: When an optimizer does its thing, it will invalidate the log being maintained by Complete Undelete or a similar utility. Before you actually run the optimizer utility, you need to review the contents of the undelete log. If there are any files in the log that you want to retain, you will have to undelete them before optimization. There really isn't a good way to resolve this conflict without making some changes in the sectors of the deleted files.

Sector Collector

Sector Collector serves a useful function during the life of your hard disk. Regardless of its quality and the diligence of your care for it, time and use will cause your hard disk to wear out. One of the indications of this wear is that sectors go bad. They lose their ability to receive and retain data without error. When this happens, your files become corrupted and things don't go right. As seen in Fig. 10-5, Sector Collector provides a window to let you know where it is in its processing. If you have more than one hard disk mounted, you will need to run this utility for each drive.

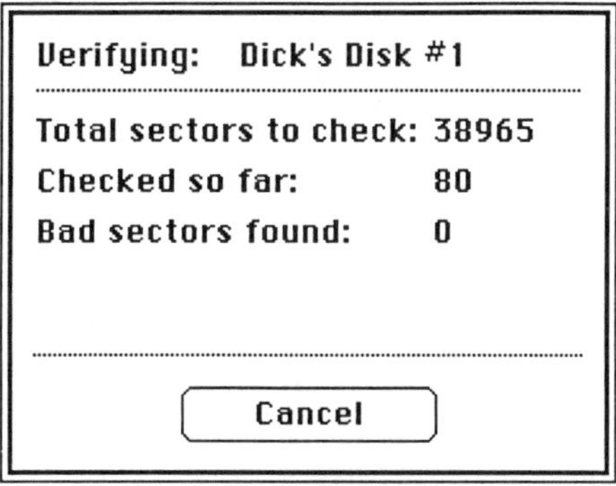

10-5 Sector Collector at work

When Sector Collector is finished checking all the sectors on a specific disk, it provides a report. Figure 10-6 is an example. In this case, there were no bad sectors. Note that there are specific areas mentioned in the report. These are the files, the directories, and the free space. The program also reports on the status of the Bad Sectors File. Again, there are none in the file either. This is to be expected, because the disk is almost new and didn't have any bad sectors when it was first initialized.

Do not be upset or imagine that you are getting bad hardware if your new hard drive has a few bad sectors the first time you initialize it. The quality and reliability of hardware is improving, but it is still far from perfect. One bad sector per megabyte of storage space isn't too much. The key is that no new bad sectors develop during the first month or so of operation. Solid

```
┌──────────────────────────────────────────────────────────────────────┐
│  Verify Report For:     Dick's Disk #1                                 │
│                                                                        │
│  Sectors:  There are 0 bad sectors: 0 in files, 0 in directories,      │
│     0 in free sectors, and 0 in a ●Bad●Sectors● file.                  │
│  There are 0 sectors that are in use but not contained in any file.    │
│  Directories: No directory damage was detected.                        │
│                                                                        │
│                                                                        │
│  Select a file:           Creator Type   Last Modified    DF  RF  Total Bad │
│  ┌ Comm WK                              1/1/91 21:15                    │
│  │ ┌ For BBS Users                      1/1/91 20:21                    │
│  │ ┌ RCMD Modules                       10/12/90 16:53                  │
│  │ ┌ Sample Filters                     10/12/90 16:42                  │
│  ┌ HyperCard                            1/1/91 21:42                    │
│  │ ┌ Help Stacks                        1/1/91 14:43                    │
│                                                                        │
│  Number of files selected:  [0]      for a total of  [0]      K        │
│                                                                        │
│  ( Recover )  ( Collect Sectors )                    ( Cancel )        │
└──────────────────────────────────────────────────────────────────────┘
```

10-6   The Sector Collector report

state electronics tend to work in one of two ways. Either they work will over a long period of time or they die almost immediately.

Bad sectors that are on the hard disk when it is purchased should be listed on a report that the manufacturer packs with the disk. This report indicates that the hard drive has been inspected and, with the exception of the bad sectors noted, has passed the inspection criteria. If the bad sectors you discover aren't on the list, then maybe something else has happened and you and the dealer you purchased the equipment from need to talk.

To discover which, if any, sectors are bad without using Sector Collector, the basic procedure is to back up all of the information on your hard disk and reformat, or initialize, your disk. The initialization program has a feature that will check the sectors and mark any bad ones. As described, this procedure takes time and must be done at regular intervals if file integrity is to be maintained. I don't know about you, but I dislike having to do 100 percent backups just so I can reformat my hard disk and then reload everything.

Obviously, there are easier ways to get this same type of file security without all of the hassle. Sector Collector is one of the ways. It checks each sector to see if it will accept and retain data properly. When it finds a sector that doesn't react properly, it marks it as a bad sector. If there is active information already written to the sector, Sector Collector attempts to relocate it to a good sector. After relocation, it marks the sector. This ensures that that sector won't be used again.

If all of the information in that sector was recovered, the file still will be good. Under most circumstances, you wouldn't even know that a sector has been relocated. When you use your optimizer program the next time, all of the sectors will be placed back in proper order and the marked sector left blank.

If Sector Collector was not able to relocate all of the information that was found in the bad sector, you will have a bit more work to do. Because recovery didn't work, it is time for rebuilding. Depending on the type of data that was lost, it might be as simple as reentering the missing letters or it might be as complex as having to reconstruct the code from a compiled program. Under most circumstances, you should have a backup copy of all of your compiled files. You will have to decide which is the better way to go: to delete the existing copy and reload another from the backup or to try to rebuild the existing code.

Rebuilding files is not always the best solution. Even the compiled code of programs that you have written can be difficult to rebuild. Text files that can be returned to the word processor for review shouldn't be too hard to rebuild. If they cannot be reviewed from within the word processor, it might be possible to edit them down to their ASCII contents and then import the remaining text.

Most users really don't get too excited about seeing all of the codes and control characters that go into making ASCII text into a word processor file. Because of this, many users are not really certain, or even aware, of what characters belong where. The loss of these characters doesn't compromise your text, but it can make a mess of things like underlining, indenting, and all of the other things that go into formatting the text into a document.

With the text complete, it will take a little time to rebuild the document. If the text isn't quite complete, it will take a little longer. The worst case is that you will have to re-enter everything. Given that you have at least a printed copy of the document, it isn't a hard task, just a time-consuming one. If you don't have a copy and can't rebuild the text, then it's time to bite the bullet and rewrite the document. Who knows, the second time around might produce a better document. In most cases, what is later seen in print isn't the first draft of the work being read.

Cache Flow

A cache is an area set aside for a special purpose. In this case, it is a portion of your RAM that is used for improving the speed of your operations. How it does this is easy to explain as long as you don't want to know how it works beyond the fact that it works well. Every time your system needs information that is on your hard disk, it must wait while that information is read and then written to RAM. Every time you want information written to your hard disk, the system waits while this action is completed.

The purpose of a cache is to reduce these wait times. To do this, the cache must make the system think that the desired activity is complete. In the case of writes to disk, the cache accepts the information and stores it, while telling the system that the write was successful. The system continues to function while the cache waits for the right opportunity to actually write the information to the disk.

For reading, the cache works in a similar manner. The first time any piece of information is requested by the system, it must come from the disk. After that it remains in the cache. When it is requested again, the time to transfer it from the cache to RAM will be much less than before. Consider that the average hard disk has an access time of approximately 20 milliseconds, while the current crop of RAM chips has an access time of about 80 nanoseconds. If "milli" is thousandths and "nano" is billionths, you can see the difference. The difference is a factor of more than 100.

Numbers this small are hard to put into a context that makes them easy to deal with. Your applications are going to get information from your hard disk almost continuously while they run. They also will be writing data back to the hard disk for later use or to provide the answers you have requested. If each of these operations (reads/writes) is performed a million or so times faster, it will make a difference by the end of the day.

The only problem with using a cache is that all of the information stored in it will be lost if there is a power interruption. For the data coming from the hard disk, there isn't really a problem. It still is on the hard disk and will be available again when the power is restored. The problem is the disk writes that really haven't been performed. The system and the application assumed that the writes were successful because the cache told them that all was well. If this information isn't actually written to the hard disk before the loss of power it will be lost forever. There is no known way to recover data lost from a cache when the power fails. With the cache feature that comes as a part of your Macintosh, a loss like this is possible. Cache Flow provides a means to overcome this possible loss. The built-in cache does its writes when it can. Cache Flow writes when it is told to do so. This is a purely manual means of ensuring the integrity of your data; however, it is better than not having the ability to ensure that everything is being written to disk as necessary.

There are other utilities that will save your current work to disk at specified intervals or when you request it. These write everything to the hard disk. Their shortcoming is that they do not offer the speed upgrade that using a cache does. You will have to weigh the differences and the probability of loss when you make your choice. It also is possible for you to have the best of both worlds. These two utilities are not mutually exclusive. Both of them can be present and working without causing problems for the other.

Minor Repairs

Note: This utility is not Multifinder compatible.

Be sure to start your system using Finder when you are going to run Minor Repairs. This shouldn't cause any problem because this isn't a utility that you are going to need every day. However, this doesn't mean that it's a utility that you'll use once and then forget. It is one of those utilities that should be a part of your regular hard disk maintenance procedures.

Minor Repairs rebuilds your Desk Top file. As you make changes in things, your Desk Top file will retain things that are no longer required. These changes also can cause fragmentation of the file. Fragmented files take longer to launch and longer to run. By using Minor Repairs periodically, you will eliminate any scraps remaining after your changes. Running Minor Repairs also will defragment the file. If you have another defragmentation utility or disk optimizer, it will perform this same function.

Defragmentation alone usually will improve the operational speed of any file. Purging any unneeded code fragments from that same file will improve performance still more. Unnecessary code fragments can cause other problems. Like anything that is out of place, it doesn't belong and therefore doesn't react properly. How this type of activity, or lack of it, will appear to you varies. Once the Desk Top file is corrupted, there is no telling what will happen. It could look like there is virus active when it is actually a much simpler problem.

When you launch Minor Repairs, you will see the screen shown in Fig. 10-7. Your two options are to make repairs or to cancel the program. Note that the Finish Repairs box is in gray. This means that you cannot select this option to start Minor Repairs.

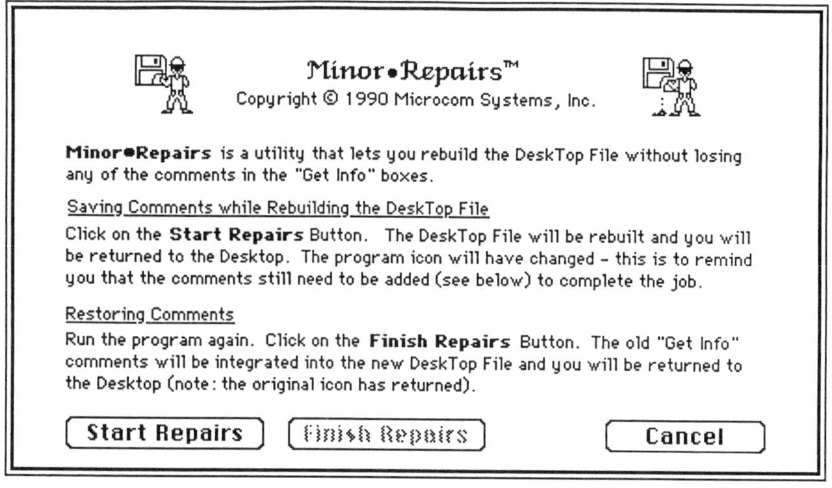

10-7 Minor Repairs' opening screen

After Minor Repairs has completed the first half of its work, you will see the screen in Fig. 10-8 displayed. Note that the Start Repairs box is now in gray. You still have the option to cancel if you like, or must, but it would be better to finish the job before moving on to other things.

Use Minor Repairs after every major reorganization of your Desk Top and about once a month between changes. This should keep your Desk Top File clean and unfragmented.

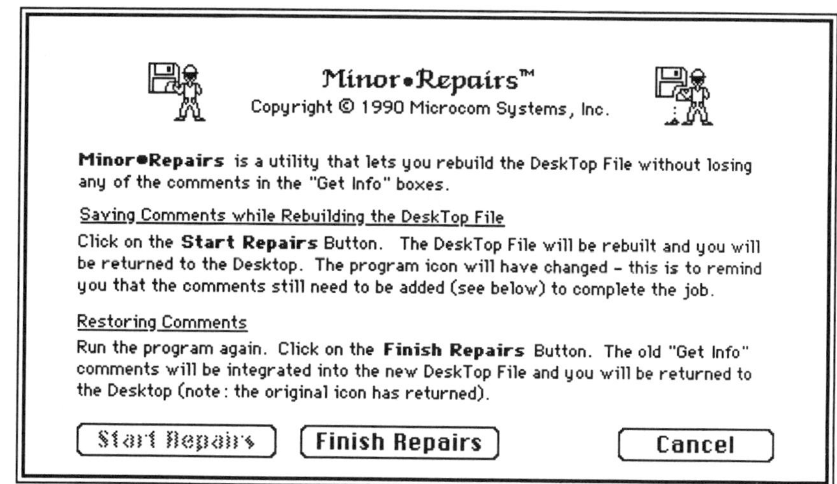

10-8   Minor Repairs' second screen

Soft Lock

Did you ever wish that there was a way to lock your hard disk like you do all of the diskettes you place in your system's drives? Soft Lock can do just that. It is not a mechanical or physical locking device like the little bits of plastic on your diskettes. It is a utility program that makes your operating system think that a device similar to that has been activated on your hard disk.

Under normal circumstances, this will ensure that nothing on your hard disk will be changed. This means that nothing is added and nothing is taken away. It is possible that a crash or an unusual rogue program will abort this level of protection. Remember it's only software, so don't think of it as foolproof.

Notice that the Control Panel (Fig. 10-9) allows you to select which of the mounted hard disks you wish to lock. Be careful when you lock things up. While you have the key, the lock still will prevent you from making any changes to locked programs until you unlock them again. Be even more careful of locking future disks. If you select this option, any disk you mount will be a read-only disk. You cannot save anything to a locked file.

One of the more obvious uses of this utility is when you have a new diskette to check out. Adding Soft Lock to the other protection you use to prevent your system from being infected will further safeguard it. This same type of thinking might bring to mind things like locking your disks while another user is

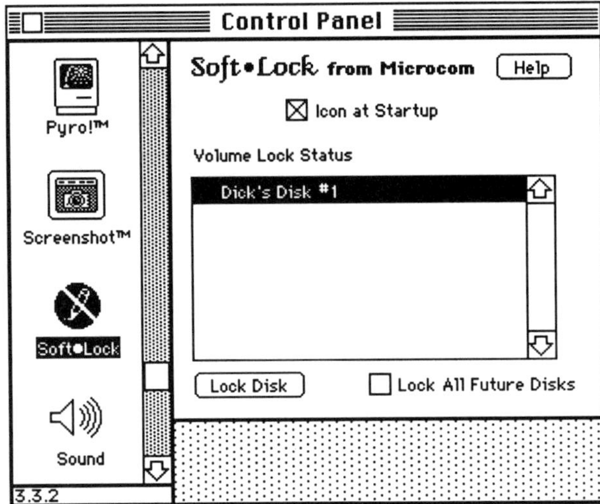

10-9 Soft Lock's Control Panel

present. This will prevent any of their errors from causing you problems. It also can be used at home to permit children to use the system while preventing them from doing your data harm.

Part 5
Microcom Software Division

11
CHAPTER

Virex

Warning: If you have any other brand of virus protection installed in your system, remove it before you attempt to install Virex. This is a powerful utility that doesn't appear to be compatible with any of the other products on the market. There is no reason why it should be, so that really isn't a problem.

Double check your System Folders a few times before running the Installer included on the Virex diskette. Be sure that all of the INITs and application programs are deleted. Failure to do this can result in system failures, which will result in your having to reinitialize your hard disk and reload all of your files.

With the release of version 3.0, Virex (Fig. 11-1) joins the ranks of the programmable utilities. You now have the ability to add the necessary information to the utility for it to search out new viruses. It is not necessary to wait for the developer to learn about the virus, determine what to do about it, update the program code and search strings, and finally get the new version out to the users. I would anticipate that the lag time between the

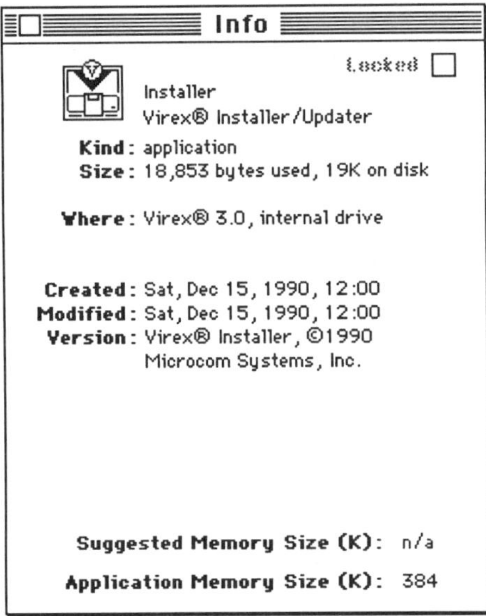

11-1 The Get Info window for Virex

discovery of a new virus and the notification of the users has been cut by months. This is especially true if the notification must take the form of an updated program diskette. Remember that only the registered users are going to get the notices in either case.

Begin at the beginning and make sure you are installing this software on a clean disk (Fig. 11-2). Clean isn't empty. It's just

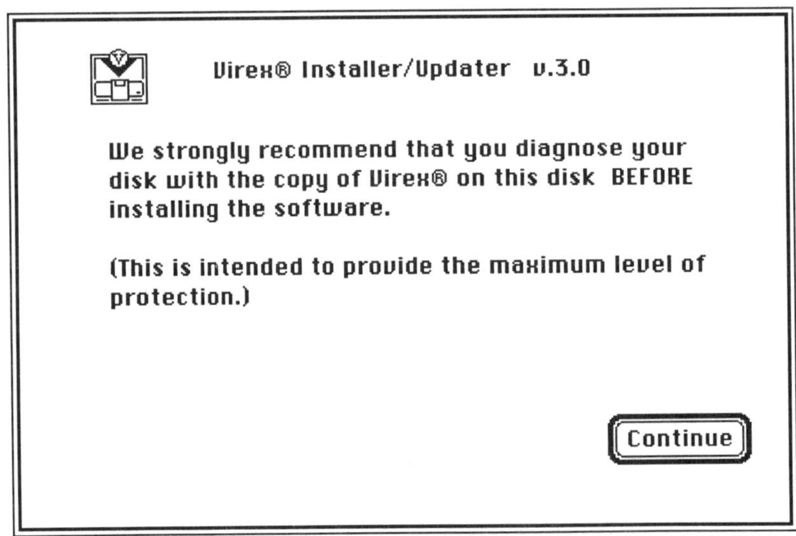

11-2 A good recommendation

free from annoying problems. If you've already done that and are headed for the next screen (Fig. 11-3) to get on with things, be sure to read before you click.

11-3 The Install screen

Be sure that you are installing Virex on the correct disk. If you are updating, the new programs will overwrite the old ones. This is an automatic process, so you don't have to do anything about the old ones. Your only real concern will be if you are changing brands of virus protection. After checking out the Virex diskette, be sure to remove all traces of the old protector before installing Virex.

Every package that the developer ships has a registration card in it. As a matter of habit, you should fill out the card and get it into the mail within 24 hours of your breaking the seal on the package. This will ensure that you get into the queue for update information and any virus alerts that are being mailed at that time. It also will get you some additional advertising mailings, but they are a small price to pay for the assurance that you are keeping your system protected.

The Virex diskette has its own System Folder (Fig. 11-4), so you can start your system from the diskette to make the initial check of your hard disk. It is possible to check this disk for viruses before you install the software, just in case you don't trust any-

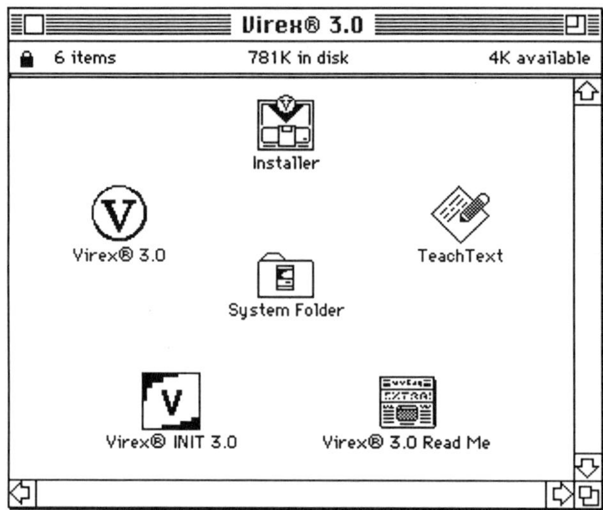

11-4 The Virex diskette window

body. I checked my copy with one of the other virus checker utilities that is highlighted in this book. As part of my test, I have checked all of the disks used in the preparation of this book at least a few times with different programs for various reasons.

The README file is there for a reason. Take a few minutes to scan it. The lead, or lag, time between the finished software and the finished manual can be a few months. This means that the developer will make every attempt to get the manual to the printer in time to be ready on the target ship date. Work on the software usually continues. Most of the changes are minor and don't have any effect on the manual or how you use the software.

There also are times when a problem is discovered that might not be big enough to stop the presses but that will make some of the text inaccurate. When this type of incident occurs, the README file grows rapidly. Most of the information will be incorporated in the next printing of the manual. This won't help you if you are among the first to use the new release. If I scan through the README file and don't see anything that grabs me, I leave the file on diskette. If there appears to be more to the file, I make a hard copy so I can read it and make notes. This is more important when typographical errors are noted in this file. One case changed the whole meaning of the sentence. There also were a few commands that were printed improperly. These made the software crash. Without the README file, I would have been very upset. (OK, I tried to run the program before I read the manual or the file and the crashes sent me to both to discover what was happening.) README files take on various filenames, which include such variations as README.DOC, README.TXT, and README.ASC. You also might find README.PRN, README.EXE, or README.SIT files. The variations are an indication of what preparations the developer has made for your use of the file.

Sometimes the file is large enough to make placing it on a single diskette, with the other files, difficult. When this happens, the developer usually will compress the file. How you will decompress it depends on the developer. The file might be self-decompressing or it might require you to use a decompression utility. These utilities are available through user groups and on most of the electronic bulletin boards. Practice safe hex with everything you get from a bulletin board or user group. They are doing the same, so you won't insult them.

The version number is easily read on the opening screen (Fig. 11-5). No need to worry about it passing before your eyes unread. It will remain in view until you click your mouse. The next screen is the heart of the program. Figure 11-6 shows that it has three parts. Along the top of the screen are the various options. The center section is a text window with a scroll bar. It

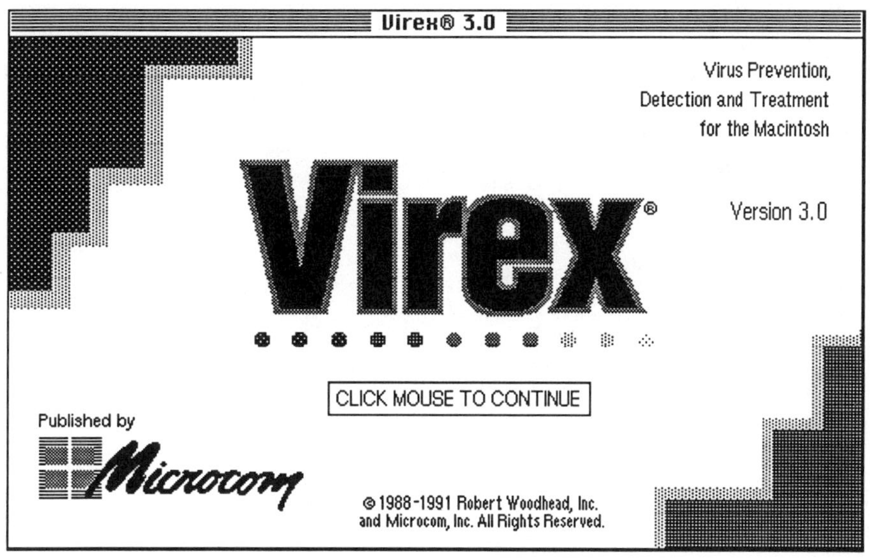

11-5 The opening screen

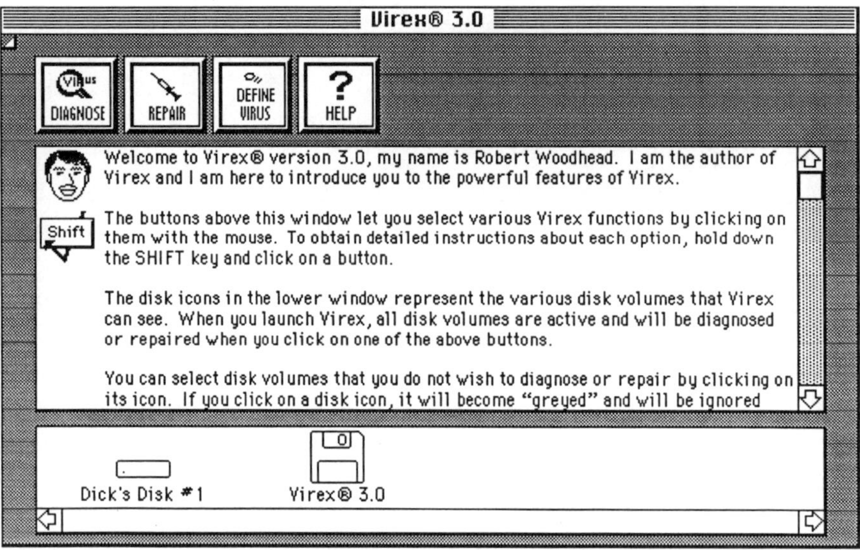

11-6 The Program screen

contains helpful information that you can read between running options. It would be better if you read it before you started doing things. The bottom portion of the screen displays the icons of the disks available for checking.

The Define Virus icon in the top row is the really interesting addition. When you click on it, a window (Fig. 11-7) will open and provide you with spaces to enter information about the new virus. Virex will protect you from this new virus after it has been properly installed and after you have verified that none of your

11-7 The Add Virus window

disks are contaminated with this new problem. Be sure to update your backup copy of the software.

The first step in the protection process is to determine if you have a problem. Clicking on the Diagnose Disk icon will launch Virex. The display changes to provide you with a status bar across the top of the screen (Fig. 11-8), a dialog area where the program's progress and problems are recorded, and the disk icons. The icon that is grayed is the one that is not being checked.

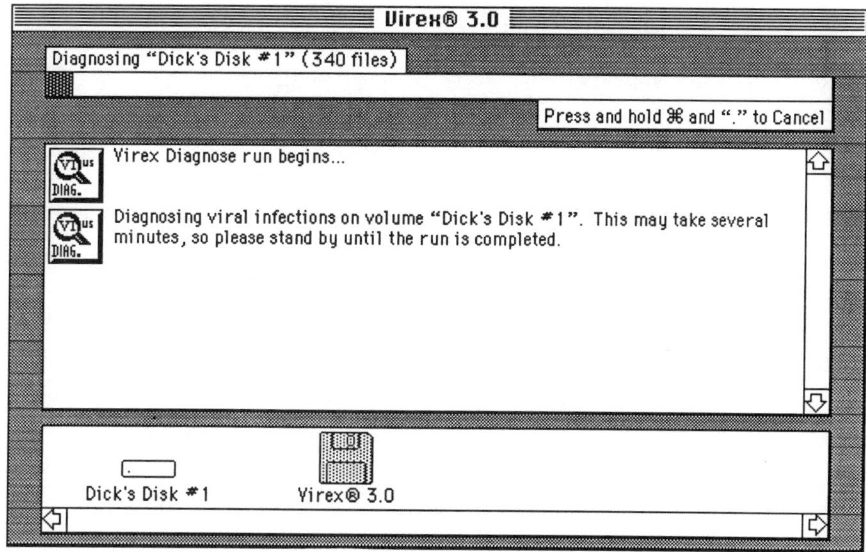

11-8 This screen is displayed while Virex is running

When Virex is finished, the results of the diagnoses will be displayed in the dialog window. If the report is longer than the window is high, use the elevator box to change the displayed text. You also can save the report to a file or just send it to your printer. Keeping the first report as a baseline might be worth the effort. If nothing else, it will give you a date when you did check your system and verification that it was clean at that time. The other possibility is that you keep just the latest report as a reminder of when you are due to check things again.

Once you have all of your diskettes and your hard disk clean, you should not put Virex away. There are a number of possible ways for an infection to sneak into your system: a diskette from a well-meaning friend, something that you get from a bulletin board, even something that was hiding on a diskette that arrived

Virex Diagnose run begins...

Diagnosing viral infections on volume "Dick's Disk #1". This may take several
minutes, so please stand by until the run is completed.

Summary of volume "Dick's Disk #1". 340 files were examined. No viruses were
found. No Trojan Horses were found.

Virex Diagnose run completed!

Volumes searched appear to be free of KNOWN computer viruses and Trojan
Horses.

11-9   A Virex report

in shrink wrap from a developer. So long as humans are involved in the computing process, there will be errors. When the computers start running themselves and no longer need humans, I'll let the computers figure out how to protect themselves against infections.

The last part of the complete installation of Virex is to work through the various options available in the Control Panel. There are only two screens but a number of options. The first screen (Fig. 11-10) is strictly advertising. Screen two holds all of the options.

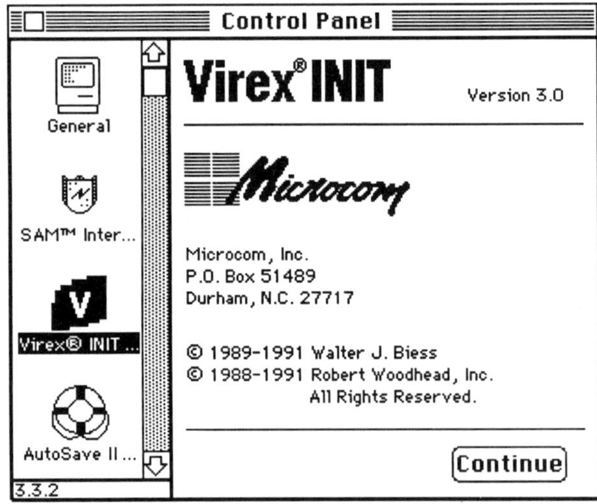

11-10   The Virex Control Panel screen

The box that reads All Volumes in Fig. 11-11 is the entry to the options. When you click this box, the remaining options will appear. As you select each of them, a new screen will display with all of the options for that selection. The options for checking are All Volumes or Floppies Only. The file diagnose options are to Diagnose files when opened, Show icon while diagnosing, Allow file repairs by Virex INIT, and Check files using record/scan data. Each of these options has a box to be checked if you want that option active.

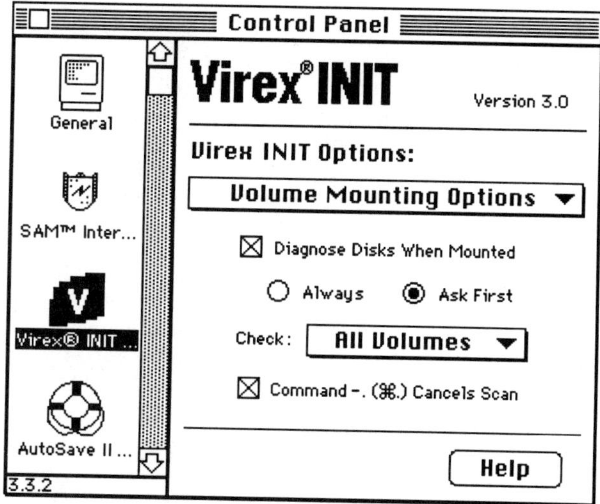

11-11 The second Control Panel screen

With the exception of the last option, all of these are recommended. The last option uses the data found in the file generated by using the Record Scan option on the main menu. This option builds a file of the checksums for each file. It then reports on any changes to these values. Because every change you make to a file, including the hidden Desktop files, will change this value, you might want to think about activating this option. If you understand what Virex is telling you each time it reports a change, you will have improved protection against unknown viruses. You will have to determine your exposure and your willingness to live with a slower but safer system. The report generated by Virex when you use the Record Scan feature is an available reference when it comes time to repair problems. Make a printed copy and put it with the rest of your baseline documentation.

Just in case you would rather read the elements of what you need to know when installing Virex, clicking the Help button will bring up the help file. Only the first part of it can be seen in Fig. 11-12. The elevator bar on the right side indicates that there is more to be scrolled up into view as you begin to read.

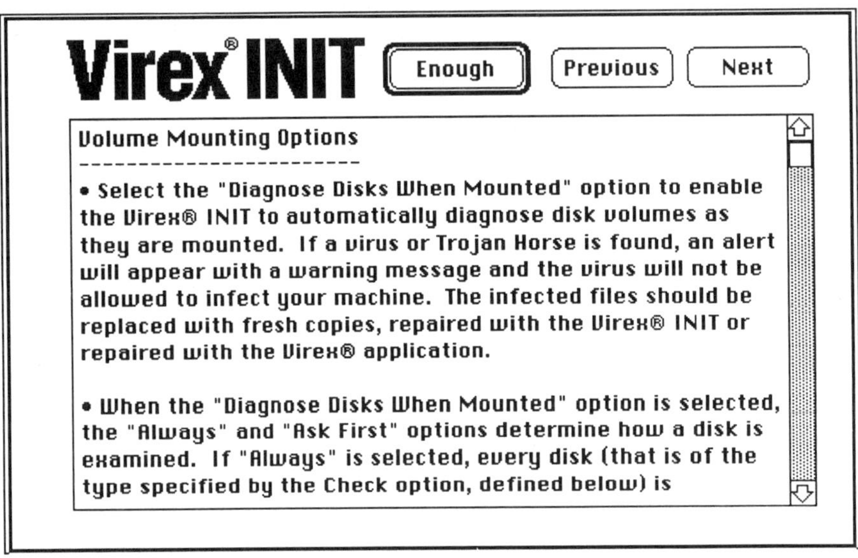

11-12 Control Panel Help

Once the software is in your system, it normally will remain active. You can disable Virex for a single session or turn it off without removing it. These choices are presented on the Installation Options screen. Another option you have here is to lock the Virex INIT in the System Folder. This will prevent everyone, including you, from removing the INIT and, therefore, your protection.

Where the Virex INIT loads can be important if you are having problems with things not working correctly. The options available are First or Last. Loading the Virex INIT first will allow it to check everything that loads after it. Letting it load last, which will usually be in the order used by the System software, might prevent conflicts with the other INITs that you use. Loading first is the recommended way to install this INIT.

The Change Password screen may or may not be used. If you choose not to use a password to protect the installation of Virex, then ignore this screen. If you feel it necessary to lock the Virex

INIT into the System Folder, you also should protect that decision with a password. If you check the box, the characters that you enter will be displayed. Otherwise, your password will never see print, at least not as far as your system is concerned. If you check the box, your password will be displayed only as long as you are in the process of changing it. Once you confirm that it is correct, it will never display again.

You also can understand that if you lose your password, as in forget, you will not be able to change any of the Control Panel settings. Here again, don't leave written copies of passwords lying around. If policy or other compelling reason requires a written copy of your password, put it in a sealed envelope. Sign the flap across the seal and place a piece of tape over the writing. This will make the password available in case of emergency without compromising it. Once the old envelope has been opened, a new password should be selected and a new envelope prepared.

The next options screen holds a nice feature. You are making backups at regular intervals now. If Virex is active during this process, it will check each of the backup diskettes as it is inserted in the drive. The possibility of your having an infected backup of a clean system is between slim and none. This assumes that you have checked your system and all of your diskettes before you made the first backup. Using the option presented here, you can turn Virex off for a fixed period of time. Select a duration that will allow you at least a few interruptions during the backup process. Even when you are home alone in the small hours of the morning, things can interrupt you.

The Set Hot Key option lets you change the default hot key to something that will not cause you problems when you press it. The hot key feature is most useful for checking single files as they enter your system. Most of the time, this will be during a telecommunications session where you are downloading a file from a bulletin board.

Setting the Automatic Scanning options is just a matter of deciding if you want to do it at all and then whether you want the scan conducted when you start your system or when you shut down. How much you want to scan will determine the length of time you will have to wait before starting work or leaving for the day. You can reduce this delay by selecting to scan only the executable files. This should not reduce your level of protection, because there is only one known virus that infects nonexecutable files. The INIT29 virus resides in data files but doesn't infect executables.

For those with networked Macs, Virex is compatible and allows the manager to set a few options that will control the entire network. He or she will appreciate the options available for establishing and maintaining the audit trail report, the network word processor, or a separate one selected by the manager. The listed choices aren't the only ones available. Virex allows the manager to add the word processor of choice to the existing list.

Networked computers present a number of special protection problems. A good policy about bringing diskettes into the office helps. It will not prevent a determined user from getting his/her favorite piece of software loaded sooner or later. An open policy where any diskette can be loaded into the system after it has been checked for contamination might be easier to enforce. However, the extra hard disk space might become a problem at some point. That point might be a good place to suggest a tighter diskette policy. Users can understand that a lack of space means that they can't work, which leads to a lack of paychecks.

Provisions also must be made for the actions and reactions Virex is to take, in the event that a problem is located. The default reaction is for the program to display a warning window. After that it waits for user/manager input. If none is forthcoming, the system waits. The entire network is down. By placing a time limit on the wait, you can specify when and what Virex is to do when a problem arises.

In the even of an infection or partial infection, Virex might be able to make the necessary repairs. This will allow the system to continue working. If all of the repairs aren't successful, then you have to decide whether to shut things down or allow a possible infection to spread. The choices available if Virex detects a change in the Record Scan are to allow work to continue or to deny access to that program. Again, this will be a policy decision by network managers. I would expect individual users to cease operations long enough to correct any problems before returning to their normal mode of operation.

Leaving an unsolved problem in an operating system is begging for more and greater problems. This type of an invitation seldom goes unanswered. Regardless of what you believe or have been told to the contrary, computers are dumb. They will do exactly as they are told. This doesn't mean that they will do what you want them to do. This only means that they will follow your instructions . . . exactly. If your instructions are not included in the launched programs, the computer will display an error message if it's able. If it can't do that, it will cease operations, or crash. Crashing systems is not a recommended activity.

The last of the options to be set is the one where you get to design the message that will display when Virex finds a problem. You are limited to text, so don't get too wild with your dreams of immortality. A simple "you goofed" type of message is adequate. This is another of those cases where you should remember to keep your words sweet, because you might be eating them. My boss is almost a computer illiterate. His business runs on and by computers. He depends on them for many things. Yet he can touch one and it will fail immediately. This might be why he has never used one regularly.

Version 3.0 of Virex allows you to add virus definitions to your current copy of the utility. You can protect yourself just as soon as you get the notice that there is another virus operating. If you are using the notification card provided to registered users, Microcom will give you the information necessary to load Virex using the Quick Entry Form. If you have received reliable information from another source or are expert enough to establish that you need to increase your protection against an as yet undefined or unnamed virus, you can enter the necessary information via the Expert Entry Form. This form takes a bit longer to complete and requires much more detailed data. If you do not have all of the information requested by the form, enter what you have and begin getting at least partial protection.

The information required by Virex's Expert Entry Form is the same information required by the other protection programs discussed in this book. You can use either the Microcom-provided information or the information received from another source to upgrade your protection. Be careful of any information received from other sources. There is a possibility that it is not correct or complete. The card that Microcom sends out will contain the information required by Virex to make valid scans for this new virus. It also will have been checked to ensure that there are no errors and that it will not cause you any problems.

This is not to say that the information on the cards sent out by any of the other developers is less correct. It says only that each developer provides the information needed by his product to provide you with the protection you expect. Using another developers information in your copy of Virex might not cause any problems; however, it also could be the last time that your copy functions correctly. My bottom line recommendation is not to mix things up. If another developer is sending out cards and you don't have one you can either be patient or call Microcom (their number is in the book) and find out when their card will arrive.

12
CHAPTER

Disinfectant

Version: 2.4
System requirement: any Macintosh system
Compatibility: Must be HFS not compatible with INIT picker
prior to version 2.0

Disinfectant (Fig. 12-1) is unique here. Like both VirusBlockade II and VirusDetective, it is not a commercial package. Unlike the other two, which are Shareware, this offering is Freeware. You can obtain a copy of it and use it without feeling guilty about not paying for it. If you feel the need to do anything, you might write the developer a nice letter of thanks for his work and the fact that he makes his software available free. John Norstad's electronic and hardcopy mailing addresses are listed in the Appendix.

Disinfectant is not a programmable utility, so, when a new virus comes along, you will have to return to a user group meeting or one of the bulletin boards where he places copies for distribution to get the new version. At the time this book went to

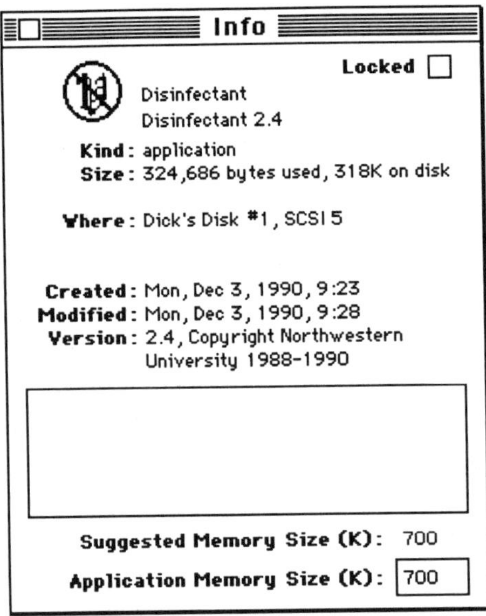

12-1 Disinfectant's Get Info screen

press, the version indicated above was the current version. Verify that it is still current before you go looking for a copy to use. If there is a later version available, use it.

The fact that this program is Freeware doesn't mean that it's a bare bones piece of software. In addition to getting a good antivirus utility, there also is a 67-page manual that comes with it. Because the distribution is electronic, the manual isn't in hard copy form when you get it. Not all of the pages are filled, but the information provided should be more than adequate for you to get up and running in the protected mode quickly.

Disinfectant (Fig. 12-2) is a detection, prevention, and repair utility. It will detect any of the viruses known to it, make repairs, and prevent reinfection by any of the viruses it can recognize. It has some code that makes it able to detect the possibility of some unknown viruses. It will not protect you from everything all of the time. What the author/developer has done is to program Disinfectant to check certain possible activities and/or code sequences that might be an indication that an as yet unnamed virus is attacking your system.

When a new virus is identified, an updated copy of Disinfectant will be placed on a number of BBSs as soon as possible. This

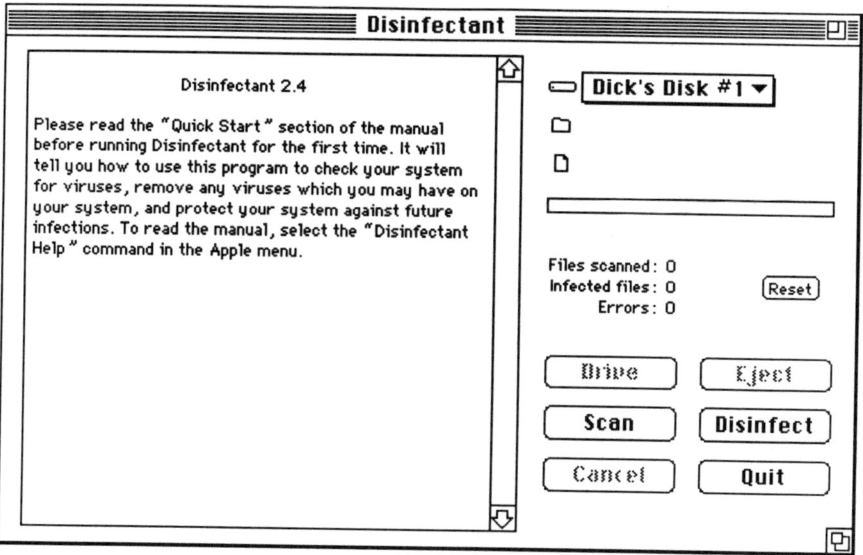

12-2 Disinfectant's opening screen

has been within a few days, according to the developer. The services that receive these updates are:

    America Online
    acns.nwu.edu.
    AppleLink
    BIX
    Calvacom
    comp.binaries.mac
    CompuServe
    DELPHI
    GEnie
    MacNet
    rascal.ics.utexas.edu
    sum-aim.stanford.edu

Users who do not have a modem or access to any of these services will have to depend on their user group or they can mail a request to the developer. His budget is limited, so you will need to include a blank 800K diskette, a mailer, and return postage.

Disinfectant is like every other virus protection utility in some ways. It doesn't attempt to protect your system from worms or Trojan Horses. These programs can do almost as much damage to a stand-alone system as they can to a networked system. Worms tend to stay in the network environment, but you shouldn't assume that they will not appear elsewhere.

There are few bells and whistles in Disinfectant. This translates into few secondary screens and only a limited number of configuration options. The needed options are there as shown in Fig. 12-3. After installing the INIT and configuring the main program, there aren't too many more things to do. One of them might be to read the rest of the manual.

12-3 The Preferences screen

It isn't too long and doesn't hide the parts you need to know in among the parts that are there just to justify the salary of the technical writer. One good point made in the manual is that, to get the most from your system, you really need to be able to access one of the electronic information services. Remote users, or those over 30 miles from the nearest active users group, are the ones who might benefit the most.

At almost any hour of the day or night, it is possible that at least one user will be wandering around in the area you are visiting. Two users make a conference and that always draws a crowd. It's nice to be able to chat with users from almost everywhere in the free world, but it's even better to be able to find answers to questions and solutions to problems. In addition to the help available from other users, there also are the vendors. They might not provide too much direct help, but knowing how to get their products might be the solution you needed.

I'm prejudiced toward one system, but I'll try to keep my comments objective. Each of the services has its own personality. Each of them also has its strengths and weaknesses. They also have differences in the supporting services they offer. Without spending a small, or large, fortune, it is possible to get access to each of the services for a short period of time. Hopefully, it will be long enough for you to make up your mind how well you like it. If you have friends or associates who use these services talk to them. After they give you their sales pitch (if they use it, it has to be the best), get them to give you a look as they do their thing on line.

All of these services are for-profit businesses. There are few free things. A few services are improving their cost per minute to the point that they are becoming very available. The lowest rate I'm aware of is the DELPHI 20/20 plan, which gives you 20 hours of access at any supported modem speed for only $20. If you run over your 20 hours, the rate increases to $4.80 an hour. With a minimum billing of two minutes, it's quite a deal. There are active areas there for both the Mac and the other Apple computers. Remember that this utility is distributed electronically. Shareware usually is distributed the same way. It is a cost-effective way to get programs into the hands of the users.

Part 7
Jeffrey S. Shulman

13
CHAPTER

VirusBlockade II

Version: 1.0. 1a
System requirement: 4.1 or higher
Compatibility: Mac Plus or better

VirusBlockade II (Fig. 13-1) is a Shareware program with a money-back guarantee. If that isn't enough to get your interest, then keep reading. There's more to come. When this INIT/cdev is installed and full protection is invoked, you can be sure that nothing on your hard disk is going to be changed in any way without your permission. It's a great way to child-proof your system, without regard to whom the children might be. You also can secure files in a public access machine from harm.

The VirusBlockade II Control Panel (Fig. 13-2) might appear a bit crowded, but it is easy to set. Just how secure do you want to keep your information and how much of this security are you willing to wade through to get any work done? It is possible for you to secure your system so that all volumes are locked and

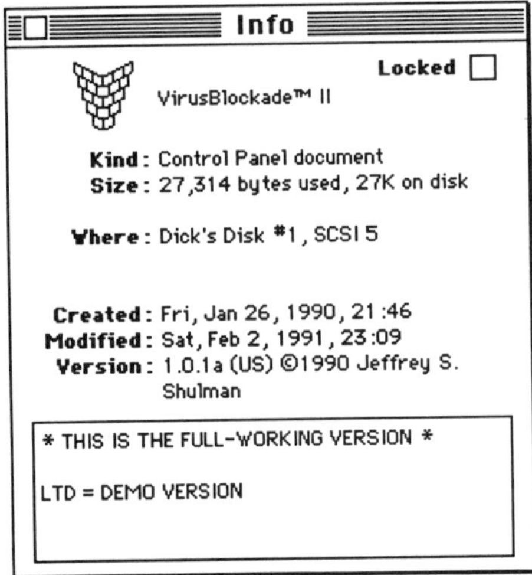

13-1 VirusBlockade's Get Info screen

13-2 The VirusBlockade II Control Panel

no floppy will be accepted. This would seem to secure everything. It also would mean that no changes can be made to anything on the disk. If you're doing word processing, that could be a problem. I make mistakes as I write and use both a spell checker and a thesaurus when I go back to proofread my work. If the possibility to make changes is removed, I'm in big trouble.

VirusBlockade II doesn't forbid changes; it just requires you to give it permission to make those changes. During some operations, this can be a useful condition. I like it when I'm looking at new software, either the kind that comes in sealed packages or the stuff I download from DELPHI. In my mind, I know there is very little possibility that anything is wrong with any of these programs. I also am aware that accidents happen. No piece of software is so made that it is impossible for anything to affect it.

By using the same technique to check out all of the software that is introduced into my system, I reduce the possibilities of problems occurring. I don't think any of the folks who have provided diskettes for the writing of this book will be insulted when they find out that I checked their diskettes out before allowing them to be copied onto my hard disk.

This habit of checking should be developed early in your computing career. About the same time you learn how to power up the system, you also should begin maintaining your system. Starting with a clean system and keeping it clean are essential. Regardless of your profession or position, you are going to find things that you want to share or have shared with you. Make sure that everything entering your system passes inspection. You also will appreciate the reputation you will gain with other users when you also can assure them that you have checked everything you are sharing. They will check your diskettes for themselves, but they will never have cause to warn others about the possibility of problems with the diskettes they receive.

VirusBlockade is only half of the software you need to provide your disks with full protection. VirusDetective is the other Shareware package you should have. Between them, they provide all you should ever need in the way of protection. This is one of the best ways you can practice safe hex.

Jeff Shulman, the person and the firm, was the first to provide virus protection utilities that were programmable. When a new virus is discovered, you, as a registered owner of the utilities, receive a post card with the necessary information to update your system's protection. You don't have to worry about the lag time while new code is written and new diskettes are made, packaged, distributed, and purchased. Before most of these activities can be planned, Jeff has the information in your hands and you are secure from harm again.

I have to compliment people like Jeff. Shareware isn't the easiest way to make a living. Most Shareware developers have to work at another job in order to pay bills. Jeff is no exception. He is available to support his products via most of the national electronic services. The information you need to contact him is listed at the back of this book. After you download a copy of either or both of his products, be sure to register them. I'm not going to suggest that you try them out for awhile first. He guarantees them for the first 30 days of usage. By registering them immediately, you will be on the mailing list for any new virus warnings that might be in the works. If at the end of the time period you can't wholeheartedly support and recommend these programs, then you might want to completely erase them off your system and tell Jeff exactly why you must have your money back.

Part 7
Jeffrey S. Shulman

14
CHAPTER

VirusDetective

Version: 4.0.3
System requirement: any Macintosh system
Compatibility: all versions of System

VirusDetective (Fig. 14-1) is a Shareware program. You can get a full working copy of the utility and try it out before you pay for it. This doesn't mean that you get to keep and use the program for free. It means that you will know what you are paying for. The developer (Jeffrey S. Shulman, the person) and his company (Jeffrey S. Shulman, the firm) are both in business. It is not Jeff's plan to be a nonprofit organization. If you find VirusDetective useful, pay the $40 (for U.S. users) or $45 (all non-U.S. users) registration fee so that you can rest easy and he can pay his bills.

I also must give Jeff credit for some of the terms used here and elsewhere in this book. His safe hex term is a good way to remind users that they must always be careful with software. His HTD (Hexually Transmitted Diseases) acronym provides an easy

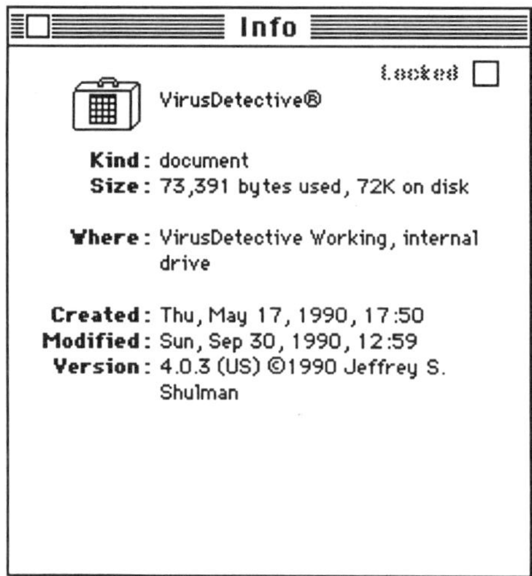

14-1 VirusDetective's Get Info screen

way to say a lot in a few words. All of this assumes that you, the reader, know what the terms mean. To make sure you do, I have put both of them in the Glossary at the back of the book.

Under most circumstances you should almost forget that you have installed and activated this utility. Its purpose in life is protection. When you live right, you don't need protection. However, with or without your knowledge and consent, your system can become infected. VirusDetective will prevent this from happening under two conditions. First, you must have the necessary search strings available. Second, VirusDetective must be active. You will have the latest search strings if you have registered your copy. VirusDetective will be active if you have followed the simple directions provided.

If you don't have the latest version you might want to get a copy from one of the subscription bulletin boards. I recommend the subscription BBS over the local free boards, unless you are personally very sure that the local board is kept clean. Compuserve, DELPHI, GEnie, On Line America, etc. have operators who must keep their areas clean, not only as a matter of pride but also their contracts with the various services tend to encourage clean software. Downloading from one of these services isn't much of a problem as long as you have a modem and the necessary communications software. White Knight is a good program to use when connecting with any of the services. Using a transfer protocol will ensure that the program is complete and error free. However, this doesn't mean that it is disease free. You should check it before you run it. If you don't have anything to do this type of checking with, you might want to consider getting your copy from the developer.

When you purchase VirusDetective from Jeffrey S. Shulman (the firm), you will receive more than just a disk with the utility on it (Fig. 14-2). Also included will be copies of Chris Johnson's GateKeeper and GateKeeper Aid and Henry Schmidt's Virus Encyclopedia HyperCard stack. The encyclopedia might tell you more than you ever wanted to know about the diseases that can infect your system. Don't let it scare you. Life still can be fun. Consider the act of keeping your system free of infections to be a challenge.

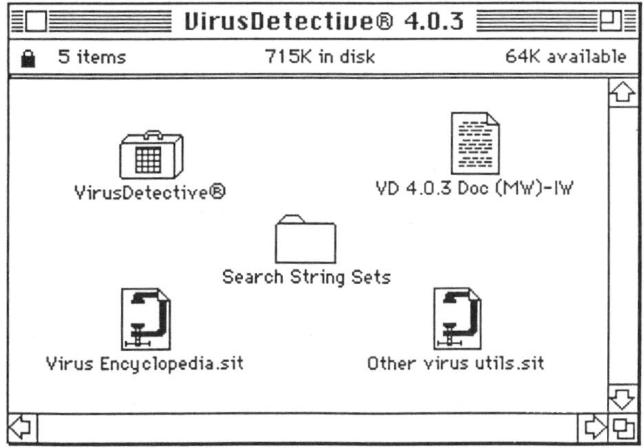

14-2 Virus Detective disk contents

VirusDetective really needs its companion program Virus Blockade II. Either can work alone, but together they will provide all of the protection you can use. If you invoke all of the possible blocks, you might find it almost impossible to get any work done. This is not to say that you have to lock everything to be safe. What it implies is that you can lock everything valuable away from harm. New users and children can do many things that no programmer or user ever considered possible.

If you have to share your system with any other users, you will want to be sure that two things don't happened. First, you want to be sure that the other user doesn't introduce any infections. You also will want to be sure that all of your application and information files are complete and unchanged after each session. You are going to be doing two things regularly. You are going to be locking files and you are going to be making backup copies of everything. How you lock your files can take several forms. There is the easy way, using the block on the Get Info screen. There are the utility programs that allow you to lock things in such a way that they can't be unlocked by anybody else.

If you think it is necessary, there also are editor utilities that will allow you to lock and hide your files. They will not appear on the desktop. If the new user learns how to manipulate the editor well enough to unhide your files, then it might be time to consider them something more than a new user. Your protection for your software from outside infection should be both complete and unobtrusive. You will have to keep the protection software current and you shouldn't have to see it any more than necessary. It also should be reliable enough that you will see it every time there is a problem or the possibility of a problem.

Remember, too, that there is more to an infection than a virus. Of the possible infections, this is the worst because you can pass it on to other users and systems. There also are things called Trojan Horses and Worms. Each of these problems has its own set of conditions that will let it exist. When these conditions are not met, the problems can be stopped and the infection will not be spread. Each user must take special care to check any media they pass on to another user. Never be the cause of a problem. When you discover one, be sure to identify it properly then tell everybody about it. This will help limit its spread.

15
CHAPTER

Symantec AntiVirus for the Macintosh

Version: 2.0
System requirement: System File 6.0. Finder 6.1 or later
Compatibility: Macintosh 512Ke, Plus, SE, SE/30, II, IIx, IIcx, IIci, and portable.
Single- and double-sided diskettes, SCSI and non-SCSI hard disks, removable hard disks, MFS and HFS file systems, and any volume on a network. Both TOPS and AppleShare are supported.

SAM, or the Symantec AntiVirus for Macintosh, is more than a single utility program. It provides a threefold attack against the problems that are caused by getting your system infected with a virus. This does not mean that you will never have a problem after installing SAM, only that the problem shouldn't be caused by a virus. You should see the screen shown in Fig. 15-1 just once on your system. After that, it should be either the screen from your working copy or the screen displayed when you open the SAM folder on your hard disk.

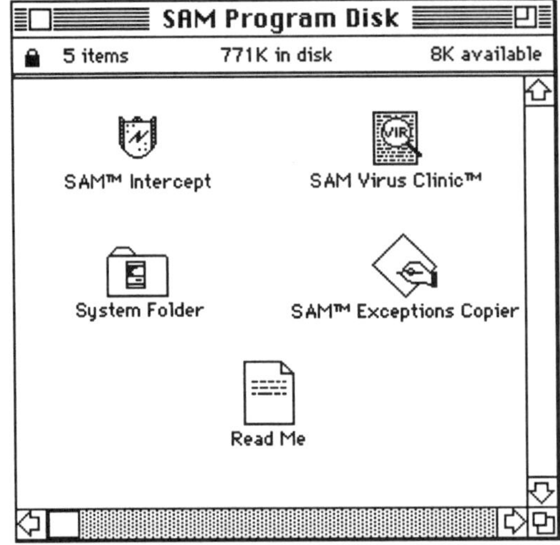

15-1   The SAM Program Disk screen

There are other utility programs discussed in this book that perform much the same functions as SAM. I cannot recommend any one over the other. You will have to evaluate each of them and determine which of them suits your needs best. Each of the utilities here has been tested by a number of users and is recommended by a number of users. You can test the Freeware and Shareware types yourself to see how they work. I'm sure you can find users in the local Mac Users Group (MUG) who can extol the virtues of the antivirus program that they have selected to protect their system.

New viruses will continue to be introduced into the computing world. This is a fact that you must learn to live with. It also means that you are going to have to begin your career as a user by practicing safe hex. Just like making backup copies of everything, virus protection usually doesn't mean much until after something happens. Be different, start with a clean system, and keep it that way. It isn't impossible and really doesn't take all that much extra time.

For those of you who frequent the electronic world of computing, this caution is most important. The operators or managers, SYSOPs, of the various subscription services work hard to keep their boards clean. The operators of the free local boards usually do the same. Regardless, problem programs still get through. The same cautions go for exchanging diskettes at user group meetings. There have been times when I've found files that I knew another user wanted or needed so I got a copy. Without even running the programs myself, I passed them on. I don't think that the person I got the files from would have knowingly given me any bad programs. I know that all of the programs that are on my system are clean. However, the giver might not have checked them any closer than I did before passing them on. The receiver of that diskette really doesn't know where it came from or what is on it. Everyone has assumed that the programs were as reported and that they were clean.

Assuming can be the worst possible thing to do when it comes to software. If sealed packages purchased directly from the developer can be infected, the chances for infection of open, freely exchanged diskettes is greater by a factor of a great magnitude raised to an infinite power. Don't be sorry; check everything carefully before you turn it loose in your system.

This warning is even more important for users on networks. More users and more drives means that there are more chances for an infected program to be introduced. The number of people who deliberately try to infect things is small. However, there are those who know they have found a virus and then pass it on for others to suffer with. I have not been able to come up with a good reason for this, unless they just want others to have all the problems they just encountered. This type of user is a far greater menace to other users than the virus developer.

Intercept

SAM Intercept (Fig. 15-2) is the prevention component of this utility set. It is the program that prevents an infection from entering your system. It isn't a living thing, so it doesn't make judgment decisions. It has been developed to perform certain functions and to react in specified ways when it encounters anything that doesn't fit the pattern. This pattern is the usual sequence of activities of a Mac system running properly.

Symantec AntiVirus
for Macintosh

SAM™ Intercept
V2.00 March 1, 1990

© 1989-1990 by Paul Cozza
All Rights Reserved

Publishing and Marketing
Symantec Corporation

Special thanks to the many individuals at
Symantec and elsewhere who contributed their
time and ideas to improve SAM.

15-2 SAM Intercept title screen

Like all good utilities, SAM Intercept allows you to make some modifications. These should help you protect your system, while still allowing you to work. Before you get to see the Control Panel, you will have the option to personalize your copy. As you can see in Fig. 15-3, I have inserted my name and one of my occupations into the proper blanks on the window that opened just before the Control Panel displayed. (I would have shown you that, too, but my reflexes weren't good enough to catch it. Also, it has little to do with the subject at hand.) You also will notice the lack of an X in the Virus protection on box. This was a temporary condition that existed while I made these illustrations and made changes in the configuration.

How you set the selections (Fig. 15-4) will determine how SAM Intercept works for you. There are additional options for each of the boxes displayed. They appear when you click on the box. They become active when you drag to the option you want and release the mouse button.

How often should you scan? What should you scan? Part of that decision will be based on how you normally receive information into your system. If everything comes in via your keyboard or a floppy diskette, then it shouldn't be necessary to perform scans after the initial scan, until you place a diskette in a drive. If your information comes in via a network port or your modem, then you might want to run a scan at other times.

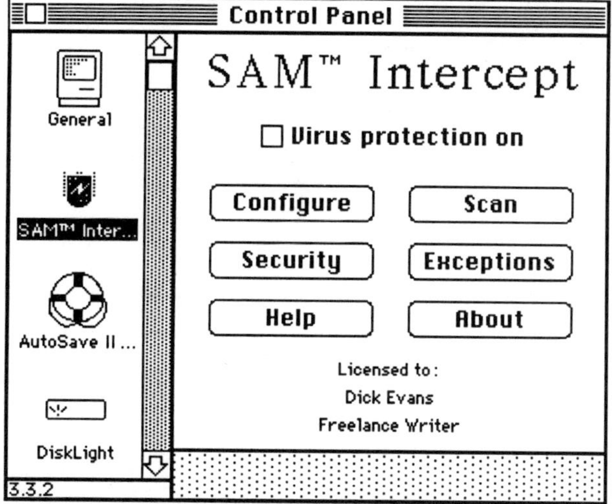

15.3 SAM Intercept Control Panel

15-4 The Intercept Configuration screen

Keeping your system clean is just as important as getting it clean the first time.

15-5 The Intercept Scan Options screen

Your single-user system might not require SAM Intercept to be locked. If others use the system, you might want to lock it so that the degree of protection you are anticipating is not changed. The words "always" and "never" (Fig. 15-6) remind me to read the text carefully for the context. Both denote very long periods of time. I've set the option to disallow scan canceling, because I don't want anything else I might try to do to abort a scan. Without a complete scan every time it's run, I cannot be sure that SAM Intercept has made every effort to protect me and my data.

15-6   The Intercept Security Options

The various tasks that must be performed on a computer usually demand enough of your attention that various alerts can be overlooked. On a monochrome system, a flashing dark prompt or window is not nearly as attention getting as a bright red window or prompt. The same applies to sounds. If there are other systems or audio distractions nearby, then it might be wise to have a special sound set to alert you to the fact that something different is happening.

Anything listed in the Exceptions screen (Fig. 15-7) isn't scanned. To me this also means that it is a gap in my protection. As you can see in the figure, there are no exceptions listed. It might not be necessary for you to go to this extent with your system's protection. It might not even be necessary for mine.

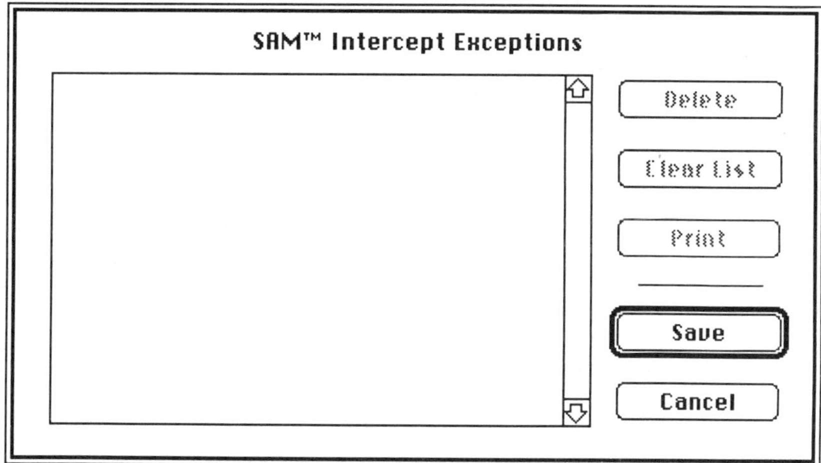

15-7 The Intercept Exceptions screen

Because it doesn't degrade the performance, I go with no exceptions when I scan.

The last two options shouldn't need any explanation. The second one returns you to the screen shown in Fig. 15-2. The help file that displays when you click on that box is brief. It is designed to get you thinking and also to remind you that you do have a manual and all of the information is in there.

New infections usually require new detection procedures. The developer understands this and has a notification system in place that tells the registered users of SAM that they need to add a new search string to their version of SAM. It is not necessary to purchase a new version of the software every time another virus is detected. You also can have protection from this new menace just as soon as you receive notification.

Please notice that I said registered users of the software. These are the users who have paid for their copy of SAM and returned the registration card that was in the package. People who steal software cost the rest of the user community money.

Virus Clinic

SAM Virus Clinic is your personal doctor. It can detect and eliminate predefined viruses. It also will create new virus definitions to detect viruses not in its catalog of defined infections. Using the update service provided by the developer, you also can add definitions to this listing, so your system can remain free of infection once you are sure that it is clean.

The manual lists a number of viruses that are predefined. This manual isn't too old (copyright 1990), yet Symantec has sent out at least two notices. One was for the MDEF C virus. The other was for the ZUC B virus. By following the instructions printed on the card, almost any user should be able to add the necessary information to their copy of SAM, so they will be protected from these infections. The procedure really isn't all that hard.

The screen in Fig. 15-8 is the one that you will use to add a new virus definition. Starting at the top, just fill in the blanks with the information provided on the card. When you have completed filling in all of the information, your screen should look like Fig. 15-9. Notice that the space available for filling in the search string wasn't long enough to display the entire string. All of the information has been correctly recorded, if you didn't make any typos, regardless of what is showing in the space. You can verify this by using the arrow keys to scroll the information back and forth, so you can check what will be written when you click on the Add button.

When you begin to configure your copy of SAM, one of the

15-8   The SAM Virus Clinic Add Virus Definition screen

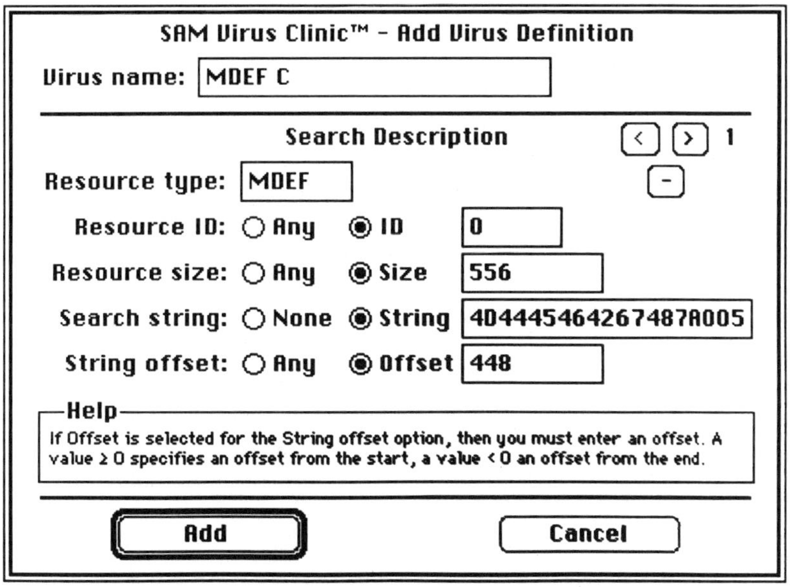

15-9   The SAM Virus Clinic screen with information added

areas will be the Virus Clinic. Because the whole purpose of having a virus detector is to protect your system, take a little time to read the manual before you start.

The General Options screen (Fig. 15-10) is just the beginning of the configuration screens. Here, you make some general ar-

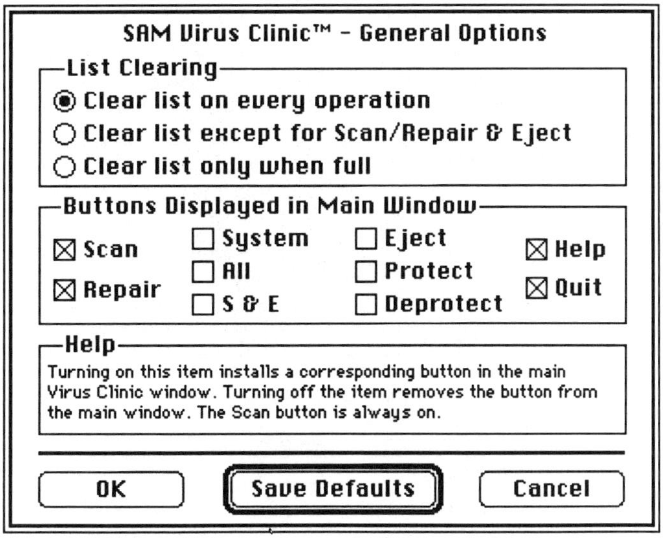

15-10   SAM Virus Clinic's General Options

rangements for how you want to interact with SAM's Virus Clinic. Things get more specific when you get into the Protection Options (Fig. 15-11). The level of protection provided by SAM Virus Clinic might be ranged from none (no boxes marked) to almost complete (marks in all the boxes).

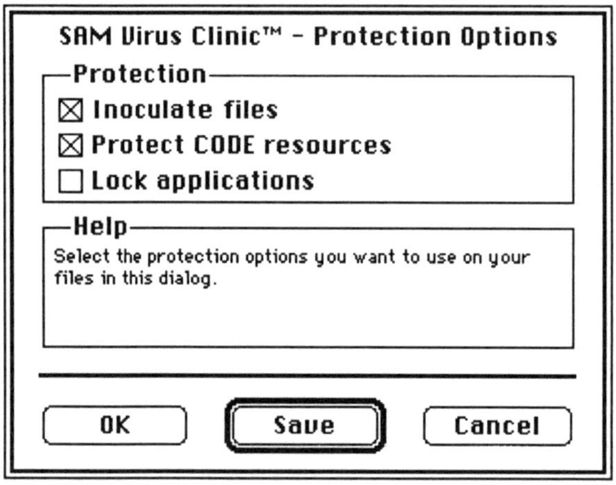

15-11 SAM Virus Clinic's Protection Options

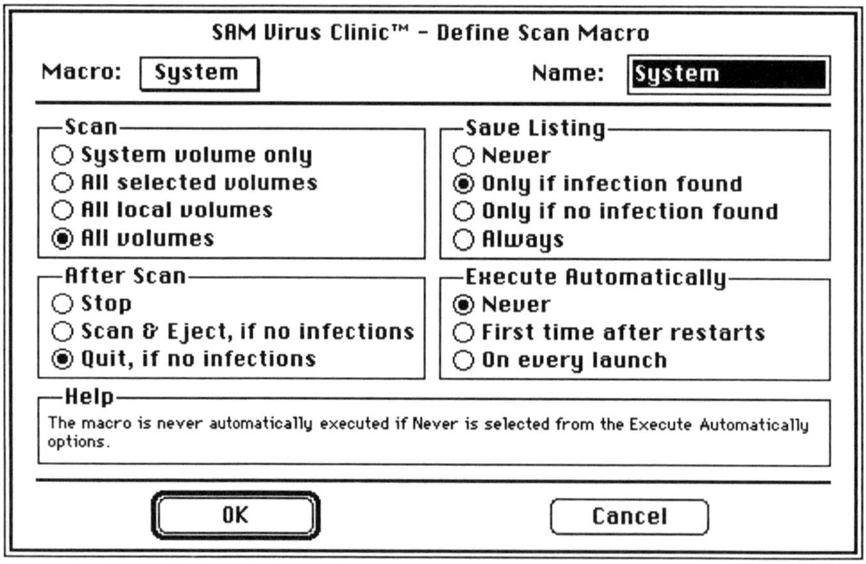

15-12 SAM Virus Clinic's Define Scan Macro

Before you send your disk to the clinic for a checkup, you need to tell the Virus Clinic what you want scanned, how you want it scanned, and what type of a report you want back. Remember that these reports can become rather lengthy, so be selective. Make sure that you get the reports you need, but don't fill your disk so full of reports that you can't get anything done. To help you sort out what you want to do and when you want it done, there are several screens (Figs. 15-12 and 15-13).

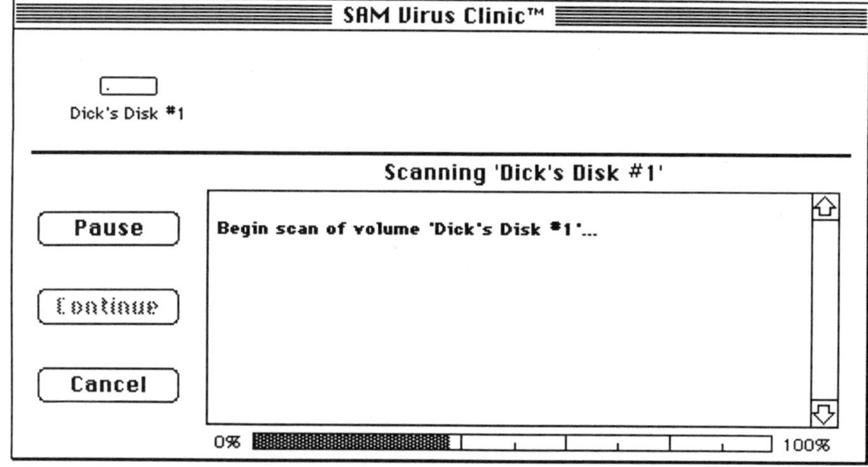

15-13 SAM Virus Clinic's Scan Options

15-14 SAM Virus Clinic's Scan screen

Now that all of the preliminaries are taken care of, it is possible to get a meaningful scan of your disk. When the scan starts, the report window in the lower portion of the screen has only the line describing the beginning of the scan (Fig. 15-14). Hopefully, the only additional information to be added to that will be that all of the files and folders have been checked and nothing was found.

Part 8
Symantec Corporation

16
CHAPTER

Symantec Utilities for the Macintosh

Version: 2.0
System requirement: System 4.1 or higher, Find 5.3 or higher.
Compatibility: Macintosh Plus, SE, SE/30, II, II/x, II/cx.
SS, DS, and HD diskettes, hard disks, SCSI and non-SCSI interfaces, tape drives.

Installing SUM II requires that you swap diskettes a few times. Don't get upset. This is the way it works. After the sixth or seventh swap, you might wonder if all is still well. Accept that it is and continue to swap diskettes upon request. It's all for a good cause: your safety and the security of your system. This disk swapping occurs both at the beginning and the end of the installation procedure.

Shield

The SUM Shield is your recovery utility. With it properly installed, you should be able to:

- Recover crashed or accidentally initialized disks.

- Recover accidentally deleted files.

- Protect your hard disk from changes, accidental and deliberate, that might make it inaccessible.

SUM Shield doesn't perform all of these functions. Both SUM Disk Clinic and SUM Recover are necessary to get the full benefit of those things that SUM Shield is able to do. The easiest place to start describing what SUM Shield does is with the Control Panel. SUM Shield is a CDEV and loads, or should be loaded, when you turn your system on. This way, it is able to provide full protection.

If you didn't read the instructions in the manual, you will see the screen in Fig. 16-1 first. This assumes that you are beginning a normal installation. The screen you should see first is shown in Fig. 16-2. It's the one with the install program on it. Right after you double click on the SUM Install icon, you will see another screen.

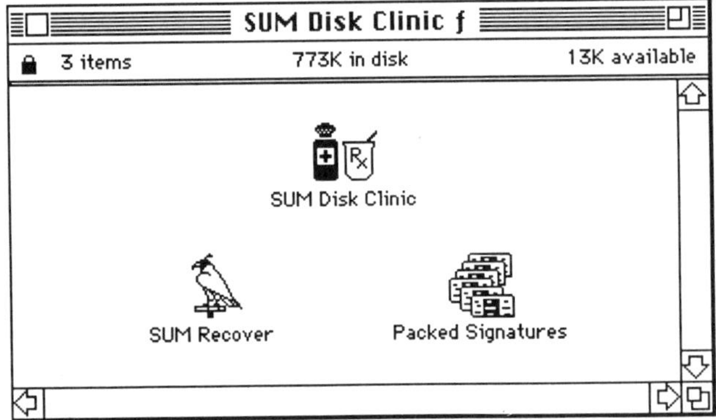

16-1 SUM Disk Clinic disk 1

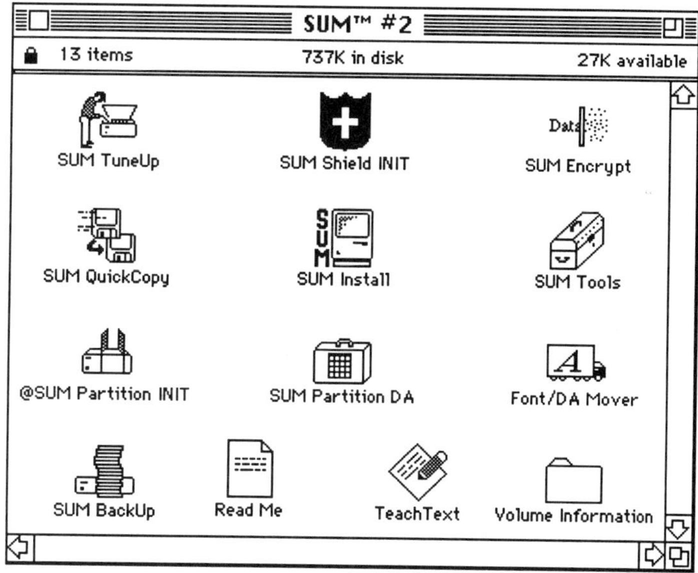

16-2   SUM Disk Clinic disk 2

Before you install any new software in your system, you really should back up everything that is already there. This will ensure that at least that much still will be available to you if something bad should happen. This is especially true when you are installing powerful utility programs, like the SUM II package. You have the option at this point to make that backup if you haven't planned ahead (Fig. 16-3). Should something happen during the installation procedure or while you are making a test run of some of the features, nothing more than your time will be lost. Your time is valuable, too. It would take even more of it to try to recover everything on the disk if that worst case should happen and there was no backup.

To make file recovery as quick and as simple as possible, SUM II keeps a record of the files you delete, as you delete them, so that when you try to recover them the necessary information about them still is available. If you have only one hard disk (Fig. 16-4), the record is placed there. If you have more than one hard disk mounted, you will have to select one or let the record be placed on the default drive. This holds true only for those files still within the deleted file record. It has only the amount of disk

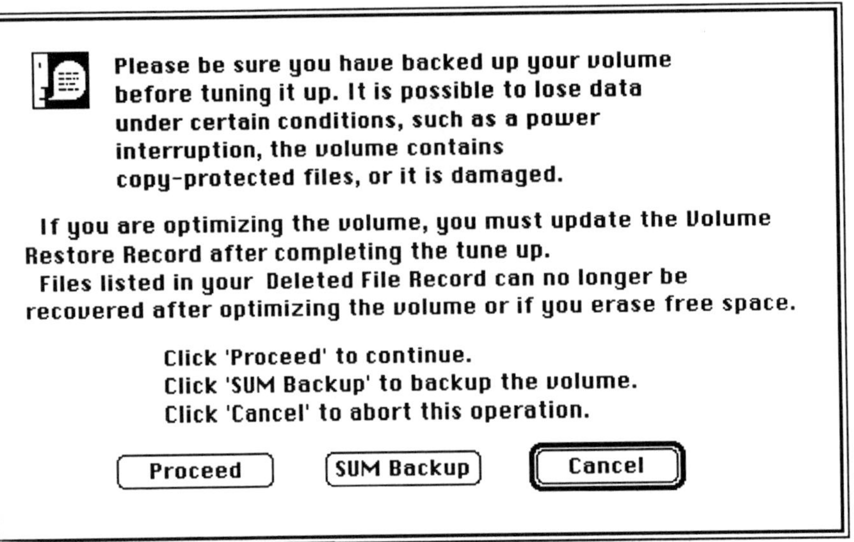

16-3   SUM Disk Clinic Warning screen

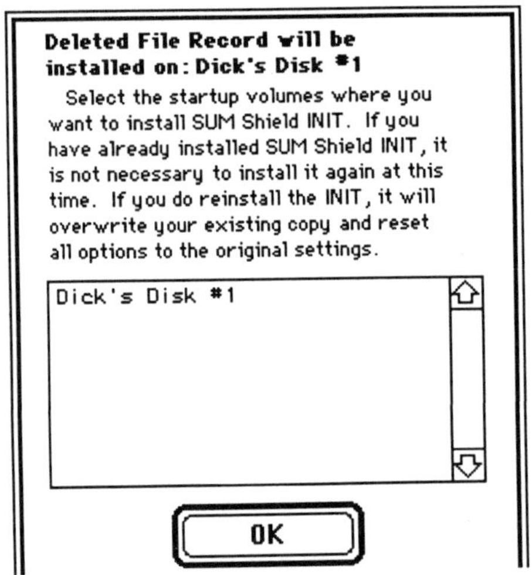

16-4   The Deleted File Record Location screen

space you set for it. When all of that space is filled with information, the utility will begin to overwrite the oldest file records first. It also will give up space if your active files fill the disk and there is no other place for them to go.

While the utility programs are being installed, the screen in Fig. 16-5 will keep you current. Both the icon and the utility name change as the installer copies the program from the diskette

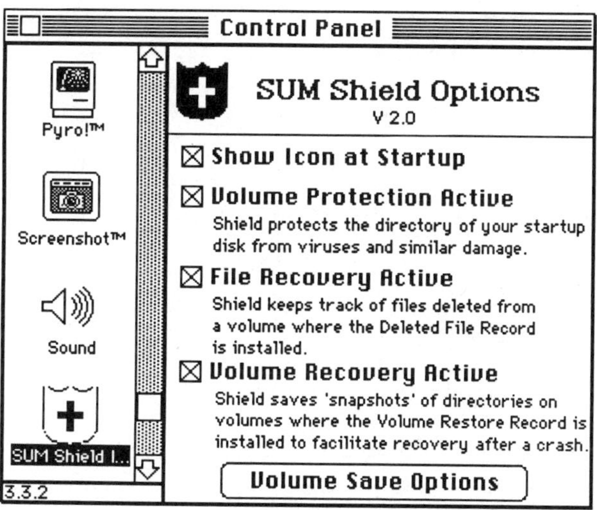

16-5 SUM Installation screen

to your hard disk. You should be using a backup copy right now and it should be locked. The only thing you should have done before making a backup copy of the SUM II diskettes is make sure that your system was clean. It is possible to make clean copies of diskettes while there is a problem present; however, it isn't the safest way to go about it. Safe hex means that you are sure of your protection before you engage in any computing activity. The final bit of configuration for SUM Shield is done on the Control Panel (Fig. 16-6).

16-6 The SUM Shield Control Panel

Disk Clinic

The Disk Clinic (Fig. 16-7) is the repair and recovery portion of SUM II. Its primary functions are to:

- Repair damage volumes
- Recover files from damaged volumes
- Recover deleted files

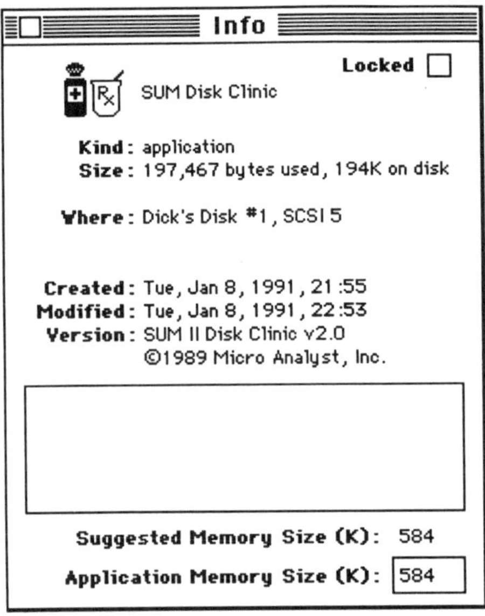

16-7 Disk Clinic's Get Info screen

In addition, Disk Clinic has a number of other features. These are:

- Make backup copies of Volume Restore Records
- Create Volume Information Files
- Rejoin files separated during recovery
- Remove Deleted File Records and Volume Restore
- Records from volumes
- Keep system configuration information current

The first time that you run the Disk Clinic program, it will automatically scan all of the active devices that your system is supporting. It then writes an internal file that stores this information. From that point on, the utility assumes that all of the devices that were active when it made its record file still are attached and active, including crashed devices, which might be why you are running the Disk Clinic. When a new device is added to the system, you should update the Disk Clinic's record file. This can be done either with the automatic scan feature or by using the manual update feature.

The record file within Disk Clinic is another reason for becoming familiar with this utility package before you really need to use it. The internal and/or hidden files created by recovery utility programs are one of the chief means they have to make your recovery operations easier and provide a greater assurance of success. All of them can perform recovery without any help from these specific files; however, it would be like trying to build a house without using power tools.

Every piece of information in a system was paid for with time. All time is valuable. To have to reinvest time to return to a place where you were is to fall behind. It also makes that information more valuable because it has cost two or three times more time to return it to the system. Application program files usually are easier to replace because they can be copied from the original diskettes again.

If the information has been received electronically, you should have made a backup copy on a diskette. The cost of connecting to the bulletin board again to download another copy can be expensive. There also is the possibility that you will have to wait for some period of time before you can connect. The lag time is another cost. I don't even want to mention the possibility that the program you are going after is no longer part of the active file section of that bulletin board. The system managers must weigh the cost of providing storage space with the activity these files generate. In the case of a free local BBS, files might not remain on line more than a few weeks or maybe as long as six months.

The subscription services usually allow files to collect dust for a slightly longer period before placing them in an off line archive. In some cases, these pay-to-connect services might be the only source for additional copies of the files you have lost.

Do not think that your backup copies of purchased programs or important information will last forever. The data on any type of magnetic media is only temporary. In most cases, the data is going to be fine after a year of storage under nominal conditions. It is going to have to be in a better than average environment to last three years. After five or more years, there is little or no guarantee that anything on the media is going to be recoverable by any means.

For your backups to be worth the time and money you have invested in them, you must rotate them at regular intervals. You should copy the data on a year-old diskette to a freshly initialized diskette. Once you have verified that the data transfer was successful and correct, reinitialize that old diskette and use it as the target diskette for another old backup diskette. With its formatting information refreshed and the data newly written onto the media, it should be able to cope with another year's inactivity without loss.

During one of these sessions of refreshing your backup copies, you might consider including the information needed by your recovery utility, so you have a little extra insurance. This concept works best with clear copies or compressed files. The files created by a backup utility usually fill all of the available media space on a diskette. Depending on your needs or policies, your backup copies could be in one or more of many formats.

When you upgrade your utility software, you need to upgrade all of your backup copies. Most developers try to have at least a degree of backward compatibility. If this doesn't reach all the way back to your first backup, save a copy of the software you used to make those backups. More than once, an organization has been faithful in making backup copies and then keeping them in the best possible environment until they were needed. When they tried to read the needed data from the media, however, they received an error message to the effect that the new software couldn't read the written data. At times, even the hardware and software that created the backup copies has been upgraded to the point that the media no longer fits the system.

Think about all of those people who used to use the old 8″ diskettes and now are into 3.5″ diskettes. The same sort of thing has happened to people who save to tape. The drives and formats have changed, as well as the operating systems. Do you have any backups buried in the back of the safe or file cabinet that might be at risk as you continue to improve and upgrade your system?

From Disk Clinic's Main Menu (Fig. 16-8), three activities are possible. Quick Fix will check your volumes for most of the more common errors and make repairs automatically. This will save you both time and effort if it is successful. Heed the warning shown in Fig. 16-9. While repair and recovery are the purposes of the Disk Clinic, it can make a mess of other broken pieces as it tries to fix the pieces it does find. Recover Volume is used to recover the files on a hard disk that has crashed or been initialized in error. However, it can not recover the files from a diskette that has been initialized in error.

There is a significant difference in the initialization procedure used for hard disks and diskettes. The hard disk initialization procedure does not overwrite all of the sectors of the disk as it places the address information in the correct locations. Diskettes initialization overwrites everything. Once overwritten, the information is lost forever. This is another reason for keeping diskettes physically locked. Nothing can be written onto the media of a locked diskette.

16-8 The Main Menu

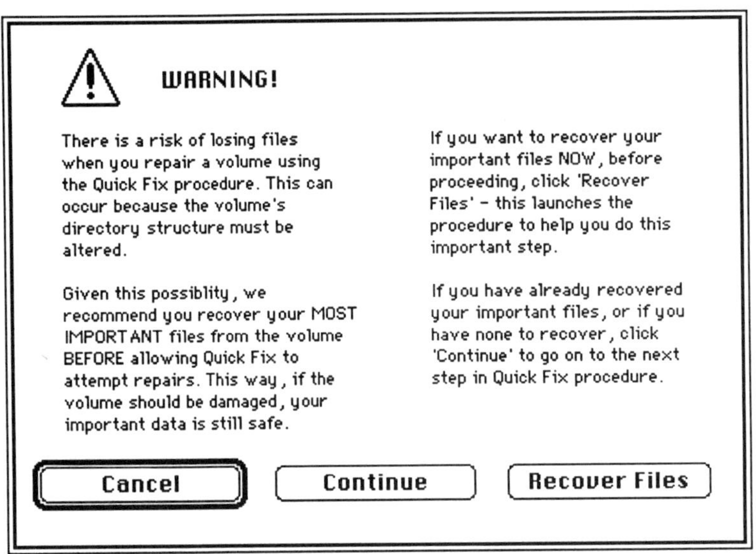

16-9 The Quick Fix warning screen

The last option is Recover Deleted Files. Deleted Files are files that have been trash canned and then the trash has been emptied. How successful you will be at this type of recovery depends on many things. Your best chance to recover a file is immediately after it has been trashed. The percentage of recovery possible will decrease the longer the delay. When there is a Deleted File Record present and your hard disk isn't full, the possibility of full recovery can extend over a period of several sessions. As your work causes writes to the disk, that probability decreases. It could drop to zero almost immediately if you use an optimizer program that physically moves the files from place to place in order to eliminate fragmentation.

If the Deleted File Record is not installed (Fig. 16-10), you still can perform all of the recovery operations. The difference will be in the percentage of files that you will be able to recover. Under almost any circumstance, a file that has just been deleted can be recovered intact. Without the Deleted File Record, the chances for full recovery decrease with every operation you perform. Don't expect miracles from the Deleted File Record. You have fixed its size, which will limit its ability to hold information.

This might be truest when you have just done some housekeeping and deleted a fair number of files. As the information is added for each new deletion, the information for the oldest dele-

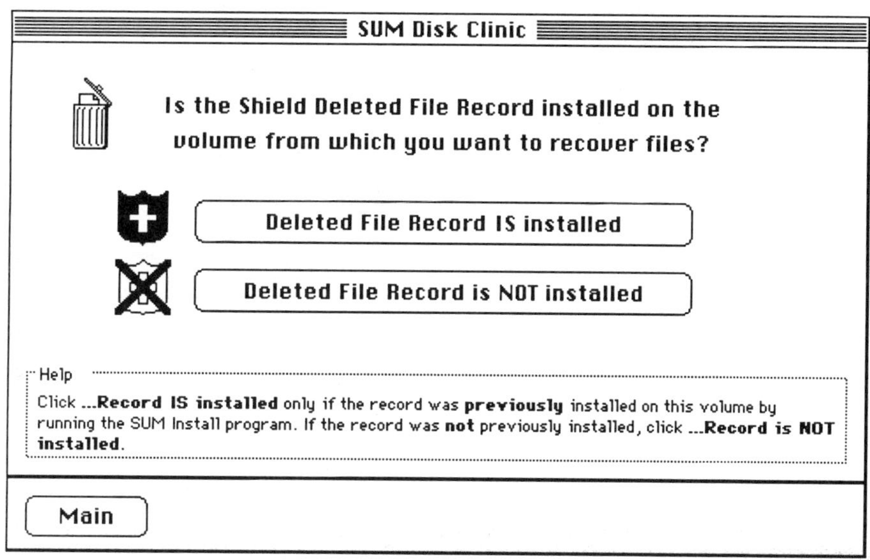

16-10   The critical question

tion is being lost. If the Record can't hold all of the information being generated by your deletions, some of your current deletions might pass all the way through the Record. Those that fall out the bottom will be subject to a lower probability of full recovery from the beginning.

Plan deletion activities and housekeeping chores to coincide with a backup or other maintenance activity. This will help to block out enough time for you to do everything that should be done in reasonable order. The biggest mess maker in an operator's life is a rush. The rush to leave or to get it done on time don't look any different to the system. Improper commands are given and things get lost or destroyed because of haste.

Anything worth doing is doing right the first time. If there isn't time to do it right, there won't be time to do it a second time. Can you imagine anything more boring than having to redo a task that you got bored doing the first time?

Beyond the first three options are a number of others. They appear when you click the options pull down. The Symptoms and Solutions Menu (Fig. 16-11) is the beginning of a series of dialogs that are designed to help you recover as much as possible with the least time and effort. Before you start any recovery operation, unless the entire system is down, make a fresh backup

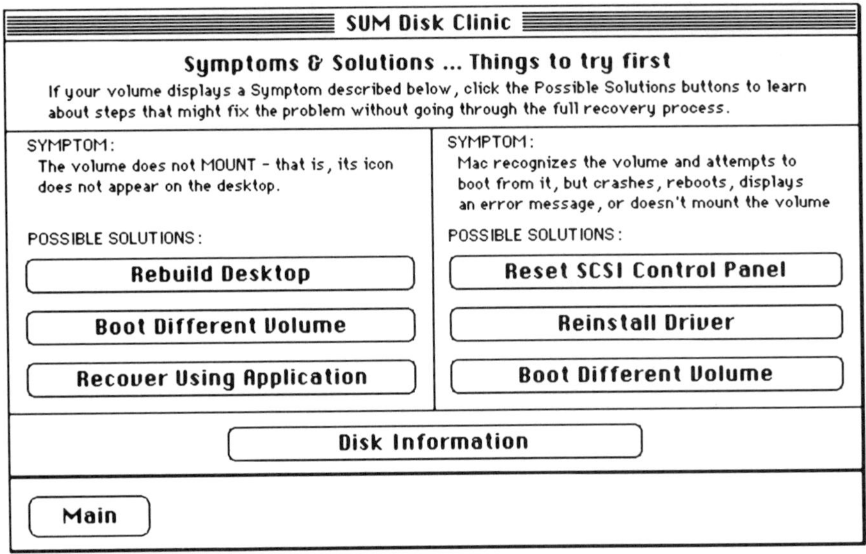

16-11 The Symptoms & Solutions Menu

of all the information still accessible. This will ensure that you don't lose anything more if one of your operations causes more damage than it repairs.

This is not to say that any of these utility programs will destroy any data. The possibility exists that additional problems will occur. In cases of disk crashes, because of physical contamination within the drive case, it is possible that a particle will cause another crash before you are finished. If the cause of the problem is electronic in nature, the remaining components might be approaching their limits in allowing you to continue working. If another one fails, you might lose all access to the drive.

Recover

SUM Recover (Fig. 16-12) is the actual SUM II utility that does the work of recovery. It can be launched directly from the desktop or by the Disk Clinic utility when it's needed. If you launch Recover from the desktop, be sure that you know what you are doing. This is one of those utilities that puts the power in your fingers. If you don't fully understand the file structures within the volumes you have, don't even look at what Recover can uncover for you. Mistakes at this level can be serious, so serious that you might not ever be able to access your hard drive again.

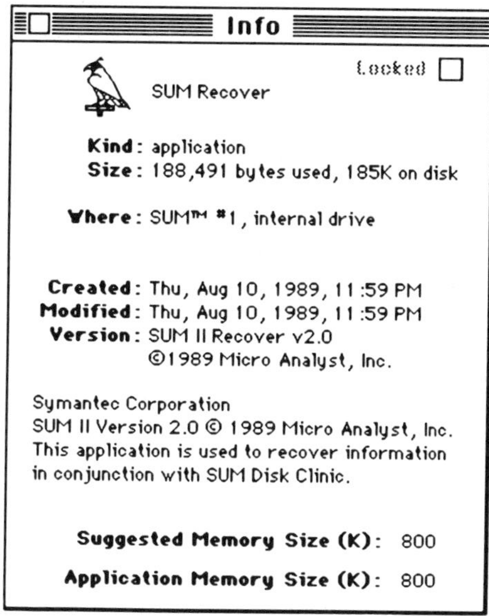

16-12 SUM Recover's Get Info screen

TuneUp

Most pieces of machinery require periodic maintenance. The files on your hard disk are no exception. As you work with your system, these files do not stay static. The data in many of the files changes each time you power up your system. In chapter 1, I outlined the way your system stores information. Over time, portions of the data files you use most will become scattered over most of the space in use on your disk. The icons on the TuneUp screen (Fig. 16-13) give you a clue as to the types of functions this utility will perform.

TuneUp's first function is a defragmenter. This portion of the utility physically moves the information in various sectors into different locations so that each file can be written into a series of contiguous sectors. After the files are defragmented, there might be gaps between the files. This could force the system to fragment the next file written to your hard disk.

The disk optimizer portion of TuneUp tries to prevent that. By their nature, some files will be changed almost every time you use the system, while others might be changed only when they are loaded into the system. Some files will never be modified. The optimizer attempts to sort and place your files onto the disk in

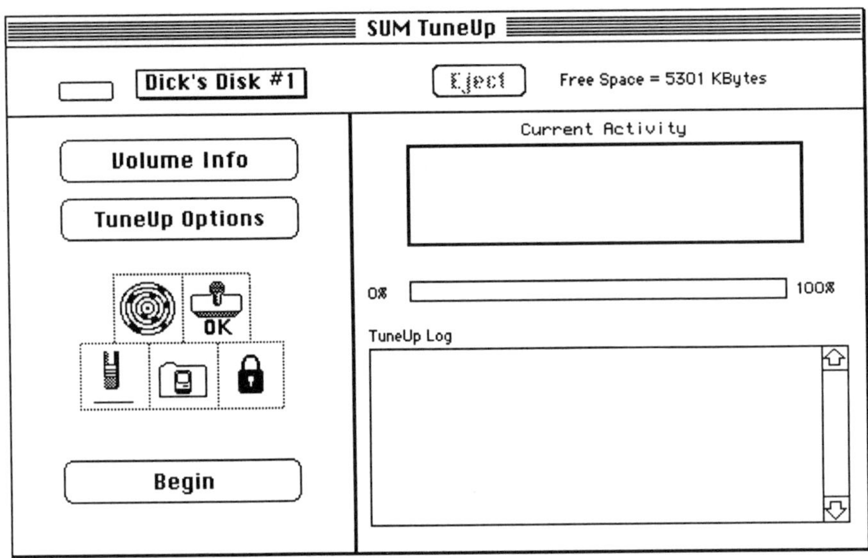

16-13 The TuneUp Main screen

such a manner that those files least likely to be changed are written first while the ones most likely to be changed are written last. This arrangement doesn't prevent fragmentation. It does reduce the number of times unchanged files have to be moved to make way for changes. This arrangement also places those files, usually application programs, nearer the beginning of the volume so that when you launch them the system can locate their first sector in a shorter period of time.

With the applications easy to find and unfragmented, the overall operating efficiency of your system stays near optimum. Good housekeeping procedures are mandatory if you are to get the maximum performance from your system. This is true from the slowest to the fastest of the Macs. Regular tuneups will take time. When they are done regularly, as in once a week or even more often, they do not take anywhere near the length of time that the first one will take. Establishing order for the first time can be a long, drawn out process. Because it is mostly automatic after you configure the utility and launch it, relax and read a book.

File data verification means that TuneUp checks each of your files to see that it has all of its parts and that those parts are in working order. For an application to work, its code and data files must be complete. It is unable to do its job if the necessary resources are not available, much like a system without a monitor. It still can run and perform useful work; however, you might have a hard time getting the correct applications launched and, if the results are displayed, you might find them hard to read. For all of the reasons listed and unlisted, computer programs are all-or-nothing propositions. They do not give reliable results if any portion is missing.

Erasing unused disk space might seem like a waste until you remember how files are deleted. Remember too that, when files are defragmented and the disk is optimized, they have passed through a massive copy and delete routine. All of this means that almost every available sector of free space on your hard disk could actually have information in it; however, it is nothing that you need or want and nothing that your system requires to operate properly. The bytes in these sectors are just the dust and scraps left from the previous operations.

The erase utility really doesn't take an eraser and go through and remove the bytes from these sectors. It simply overwrites each sector with a value. The number one or a zero are the most common. Any value or combination of values can be used. It also is possible to change the value used with each pass. Multiple passes are not routine. A single pass using a value of one or zero should be adequate.

Another utility routine in this package is one designed to identify and isolate bad sectors. By locking out these sectors, you are assured that you should be able to read all of the information you write to your disk. This is another of those utilities that should become a part of your regular housekeeping maintenance procedure. It doesn't take all that long to run and it does reduce the possibilities of current problems. It also is a good indicator of possible trouble to come.

A hard disk should not have many bad sectors when you purchase it. During its useful life, it should not develop many more. Toward the end of that lifetime, it might begin to develop more bad sectors before its final crash. So, if you start seeing this utility finding and marking bad sectors almost every time you run it, be warned. There are other reasons that a piece of software will think a piece of hardware is not responding correctly. Regardless of the reason for the report of more bad sectors, you should become cautious about what you do with your system until the exact cause can be determined. Obviously, determining the cause of the problem is only half of the job. To finish it, you must correct the problem. In the case of old hard disks, it usually means that they must be shipped back to the manufacturer for rebuild or replacement. You had best have a copy of all the information left on the disk before it leaves. The disk you receive in return will not have your information on it.

The report provided by TuneUp (Fig. 16-14) will help you determine the state of your hard disk. Making a report just after you get everything organized on your system to use as a baseline will help later when you are trying to determine what has changed. The length and contents of the reports will differ according to the contents of the disk.

16-14 The TuneUp report

```
Volume -> Dick's Disk #1

Sat, Apr 13, 1991  11:21 PM

- - - - - - - - - - - - - - - - - - - - - - - - - - - - - - - - - - - - - -

Verifying  Files


Number of files on volume -> 319
Number of files verified -> 319

Verify Files – DONE

- - - - - - - - - - - - - - - - - - - - - - - - - - - - - - - - - - - - - -

List all INITs in system folder.

INITs in System file

INIT ID  0     Keyboard INIT
INIT ID  1     Keyboard INIT
INIT ID  4
INIT ID  5
INIT ID  6
INIT ID  10
INIT ID  11
INIT ID  22
INIT ID  30
INIT ID  31     INIT Loader
INIT ID  35     Caching INIT
INIT ID  3      q
```

INIT ID 29

 Other INITs in system folder

CDEV (Control Panel) file -> AutoSave II 1.11

INIT ID 129 AutoSave II

Lock Out Bad Sectors

Lock Out Bad Sectors – DONE

Erase Free Space

Erase Free Space – DONE

Defragmenting files.

Scanning disk. Total number of files: 319

Defragmenting -> System
Unable to defragment, File is open.

Defragmenting files – DONE

TuneUp – DONE

 CDEV (Control Panel) file -> DiskLight

INIT ID 128 DiskLight™

INIT file -> Easy Access

INIT ID 1 Sticky Keys
INIT ID 2 ADB Sticky Keys
INIT ID 3 Mouse Keys

CDEV (Control Panel) file -> FileSaver

INIT ID 128 File Saver™

16-14 Continued

CDEV (Control Panel) file -> MasterStrokes

INIT ID 0 MasterStrokes

CDEV (Control Panel) file -> Pyro!™

INIT ID 128 Pyro!

CDEV (Control Panel) file -> Screenshot™

INIT ID 12 ScreenShot™ INIT

INIT file -> Suitcase™ II

INIT ID 128

CDEV (Control Panel) file -> VirusBlockade™ II

INIT ID 0

Number of INITs found -> 25

List INITs - DONE

BackUp

SUM BackUp (Fig. 16-15) is another utility that performs backups. Read through the features and see if they meet your needs. You must have a good means to backup your files. You also need a good way to restore them. BackUp is that type of utility. It gives you various options for making your backups. You can back up everything, just your applications, or just your documents of selected files or folders. You also can restore anything you can back up.

After you make a full or complete backup of everything, BackUp can use the BackUpSet file that it created to make incremental backups until you either have to do a restore or you feel that it's time to make another complete backup. An incremental backup is a backup of only those files that have been changed since the last complete or incremental backup. A file that is worked on every day will be backed up every evening, assuming that you backup before shutting down for the night.

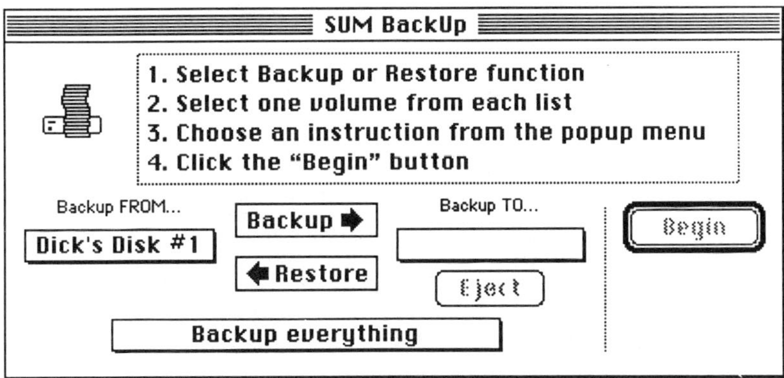

16-15 SUM Backup Main screen

Incremental backups retain the changes made each day, which will allow you to track changes or chart progress. It also can tell you when something got lost. An incremental backup differs from an differential backup, which always backs up everything that has been changed since the last complete backup. A differential backup also will overwrite the older differential backups. You have lost your record of changes, but not the end result. With just the last differential backup and the complete backup, you can restore all of your files to currency. With incremental backups, you would need every one of the increments plus the last complete backup. You also would have to reload all of the incrementals so that you could be sure that all of the changes are posted to the disk files before you start work again.

BackUp keeps its log file on the first diskette. It will be loaded as soon as you run that diskette. You will have to place that first diskette back into the drive when the backup is complete so that the log can be updated. It is possible to restore the files on that backup without the log; however, it will take longer and there is always the possibility of an error that prevents everything from being restored. In everything you do regarding security, backups, restoration, and recovery, the primary need is for attention to detail, all of the details.

Partition

Hard disks with up to 40Mb or so as a single volume are manageable. When they get larger, things tend to get lost. Backing up these larger drives also presents its own special set of problems to be solved.

Diskettes are not the way to go when you have a number of large drives. The easiest means is tape. You can use either the smaller footprint models, which will hold up to about 40Mb of data, or the larger file-server type, which will hold hundreds of megabytes of data. All of the later model tape drives have some form of data compression, so they can hold more information on the same small tape.

When it comes time to delete a partition, be sure it is empty. If it isn't empty, be ready to lose all of the files that are in that partition. If you need the files but do not have room on one of your hard disks to copy the files out of the partition, you will need to copy them, or make a backup, to floppy diskettes. After the partition is deleted, the space will be available for your use again.

In addition to being able to manage your system more efficiently, Partition has some other useful features. The basic partition software is hard and floppy diskette compatible. This means that you can put multiple volumes on a single diskette. Until the 1.44 Mb diskettes, this might not have seemed as important a feature. These new diskettes can hold almost as much as two of the older 800K diskettes. With file compression, they might be able to hold even more.

Another feature present in this utility will be useful to some. Partition allows you to encrypt files. Encryption scrambles the information in a file so that another user cannot read it. It also prevents other users from being able to use an application or any other program that is transformed with this security device.

If you use the features of Partition, be sure that the icon appears when you start your system. If the INIT doesn't load, the icon doesn't display. If it isn't loaded, you will not be able to access your partitions. This can be a real problem. Remember that you are limited to 15 INITs active at any one time. If you have more than that available, you need to have a means of keeping them separated so that no more than 15 are loading at any one time.

QuickCopy

SUM QuickCopy is a fast floppy-to-floppy copy routine. It will not copy files to or from your hard disk. It also can be used to initialize a group of floppy diskettes quickly. Both source and target diskettes must be of the same type. You can copy from any of the formats your drive will read to any of those same formats only. If your drive cannot read a format correctly, do not attempt to use QuickCopy to make a copy of that diskette. A little prior planning will reduce the frustration of learning about the limitations of this program by the error and error method.

Be sure to keep your source diskettes locked when using QuickCopy. It doesn't check to determine which diskette is in the drive before it copies the files in RAM to that diskette. If you have a source diskette in the drive, all of the information on it could be overwritten. Overwritten information is not recoverable. (A locked diskette is one where you can see through the small hole on the left side as seen when the diskette is ready to be placed in a drive.)

The quickest way to copy a diskette using QuickCopy is to copy only the sectors in use on the source or master diskette. Unless all of the sectors on the master actually contain information, the amount of system memory needed to hold the files will be less and the time it takes to transfer this information to the target or copy diskette will be correspondingly less. For systems with RAM limitations, this usually is the more efficient way to make copies.

Being able to copy software doesn't mean that you are authorized to give away or sell that software. The only exceptions are programs that you have developed. Shareware also can be copied legally for farther distribution without breaking any laws. If the files on your source diskette are copy protected in any way, QuickCopy will not copy the diskette. It will abort and report an error message.

Encrypt

Note: Encrypt will not encode application files.

There are two methods available to encrypt files. They are the Data Encryption Standard (DES) method and all others. The

DES method was developed by the United States Bureau of Standards. Each of the others has been generated by their developer as an alternate to the DES method. The individual developer's methods usually are faster and unique to that utility. The DES method must meet certain standards; however, compatibility is not one of them. While they might or might not use any of the same algorithms in the same way, they are not required to be compatible with another developer's DES standard package.

You will have to be certain that the receiver of any encrypted files you send out has a copy of SUM II and the Encrypt utility. For most conventional security requirements, the proprietary method used by Encrypt should be adequate. Where policy or law require a greater degree of security use the DES method. Just be sure that all of this security isn't compromised by failing to protect the password.

Having a password without knowing which file it belongs to might seem to be of little real value. This is untrue when the list of words is in the hands of an individual or organization that would like to be able to read your files. By default or design, your password lists will fit a pattern. Once this pattern is defined, it is possible for a computer program to be written that will generate more passwords. With this expanded list the possibility of breaking into your files increases greatly. Think about that when you decide to write a program to generate passwords for your personal or organizational use. The password list sequence has little, if any, bearing on the matter. The important points are the length and the character sequence. To make it as hard as possible to break, your passwords should use all of the available characters in every one of the positions.

Random sequences of letters, numbers, and symbols might be the hardest to break; however, they also are the hardest to memorize. There is no easy way out of this corner. Any of the easy solutions you can generate will either compromise the security you are trying to achieve or will eliminate the security you require. Just like the requirement to change passwords from time to time helps enhance security, it also creates problems for the users. They have to memorize a new password. Again, cooperation and continuous attention to every detail are required for any security system to work.

Tools

SUM Tools (Fig. 16-16) is the experts utility. With it, you have access to everything on a disk or diskette (Fig. 16-17). Tools overwrites when it makes changes. After you have made a change, whatever was there is no longer present. If you aren't sure what to do, your best course of action is not to do anything. If you are in a situation where you have to do something, use a copy of the file. This way, you will be able to make changes without creating a greater problem. Access to the rest of the menus and information is via the Mac Info bar in the upper right portion of the screen.

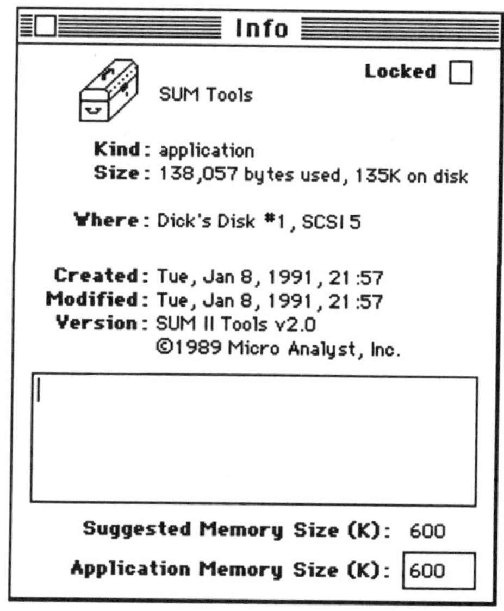

16-16   SUM Tools Get Info screen

The first screen (Fig. 16-18) tells you about your system. This screen begins to get into the details. Where before you were told that you have a number of kilobytes of RAM, this screen tells you how it is being utilized. The balance of the screens get even more detailed. They are the ones where you can do your editing. Remember that editing here is overwriting.

With this warning in mind, there are some of the Tools that still are useful to even the most novice of users. Without attempting to do any editing, there are a number of information windows available to tell you all about the object you are check-

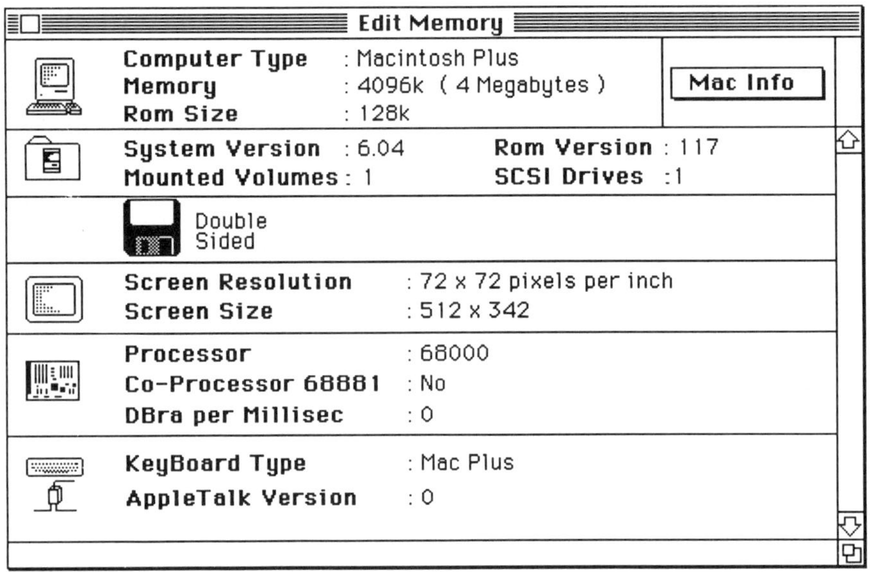

16-17 The SUM Tools screen

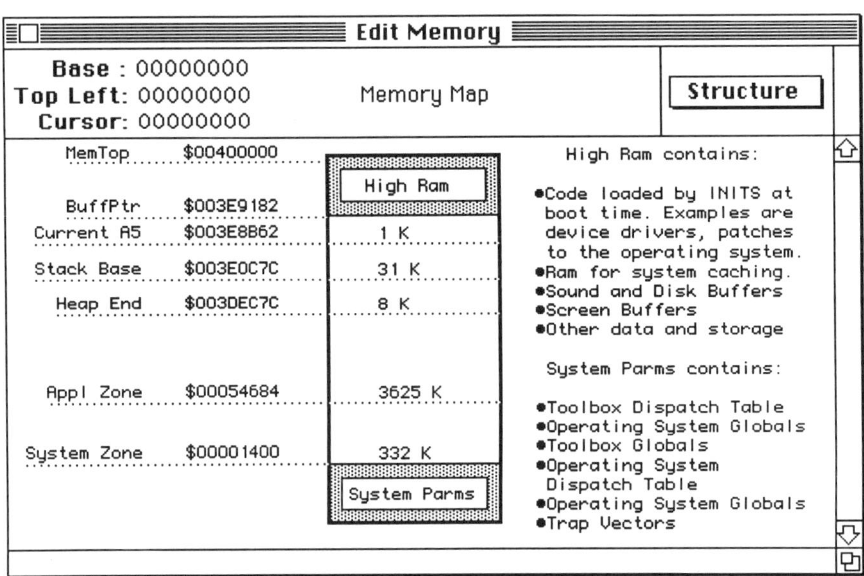

16-18 The Memory Info screen

ing. You do not have the ability to edit in an information window, so there is little possibility of doing any damage.

Using the map windows, you can determine where the various files are stored on your disks. This might or might be of interest under most conditions, but it will give you a graphic representation of the condition of your disks. The white gaps between files are free space. This usually is an indication of fragmentation in your files. It also means that when you write files to your disks, they too might become fragmented rather quickly.

Fragmentation isn't something that will cause your system not to work. It will require your system to work a bit harder than normal. An unfragmented file can be read into memory with a minimum of movement by the read/write head of the disk drive. Jumping around to find all of the sectors that are the file provides a possibility for errors. The same thing is true when the system is forced to write into noncontiguous sectors.

The disk drives are mechanical devices. They wear out over time. This wear can be accelerated by poor housekeeping habits. Another result of fragmentation appears when you are trying to recover files. When they are fragmented, you might have to search the entire disk to locate the next sector in the sequence. By keeping both the files and the free space unfragmented, you will reduce the time it takes for system operations. There also will be a reduction in the frustration you feel when you are trying to find a specific sector.

For the really adventurous user, there is the DISAM window. This feature of Tools displays a program in assembly language format. Short of going to the basic ones and zeros of true machine language, this is about as low as you can get in computer languages. Low-level programming is not easy. For those who know how to do it, assembler is a powerful and efficient language. If it is necessary to work at this level, try to do so using the tools available in your language compiler package. If this isn't possible, then work on a copy of the program. Tools doesn't have the logic checkers and other enhancements that usually are built into the compiler tool programs.

Tools isn't designed for the programmer/developer to use as a development aid. Its purpose in life is to aid the technician with repairs and recovery operations. Used as it was designed, it is a powerful tool. Its capacity for abuse is as great as its power to repair. Don't be a victim of the abuse of power. Be careful and pay attention to every detail, all of the time. Tools can not be used in haste or by those who have no idea what's happening when they start doing things.

17
CHAPTER

Norton Utilities for the Macintosh

Version: 1.0
System requirement: System 4.2 through 6.0.4
Compatibility: Macintosh Plus, SE, SE/30, II, IIx, IIcx, IIci & Portable

The Norton Utilities are well-known in the DOS world. They have proven themselves over time. The Peter Norton Computing Group also has proven itself during this same period. They have always maintained a well-trained technical support staff, and their programmers have consistently written excellent utility programs. This can be verified by looking at the various ads for DOS hardware. When the manufacturer wants to make a speed claim about his product, he usually quotes a decimal figure that has been generated by the Norton Utility System Information. This is not a utility currently available for the Mac. It also is a utility that will not become available for the Mac because there aren't any Mac clones on the market.

Some of the utilities (Fig. 17-1) presented here have a counterpart in the DOS world. Others are unique to the Macintosh world. As they are presented, you will understand why this difference exists.

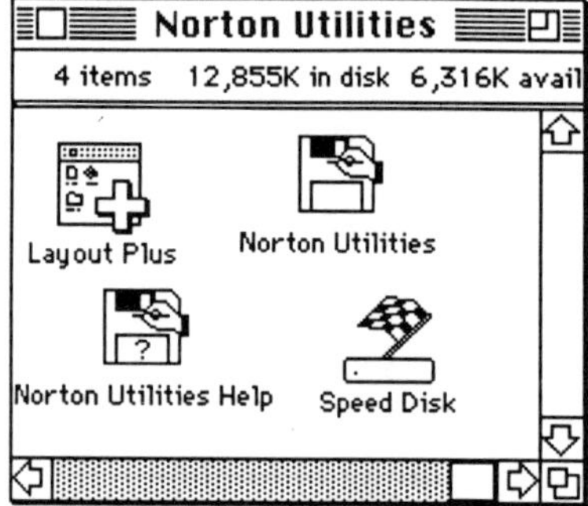

17-1 Norton On the desktop

There are a number of useful pieces of information available in the help files. They are organized in a logical manner, so you don't have to dig for hours to find a minute's worth of information. Figure 17-2 illustrates the Topics screen. Select the one you want to get more information about and it will be displayed.

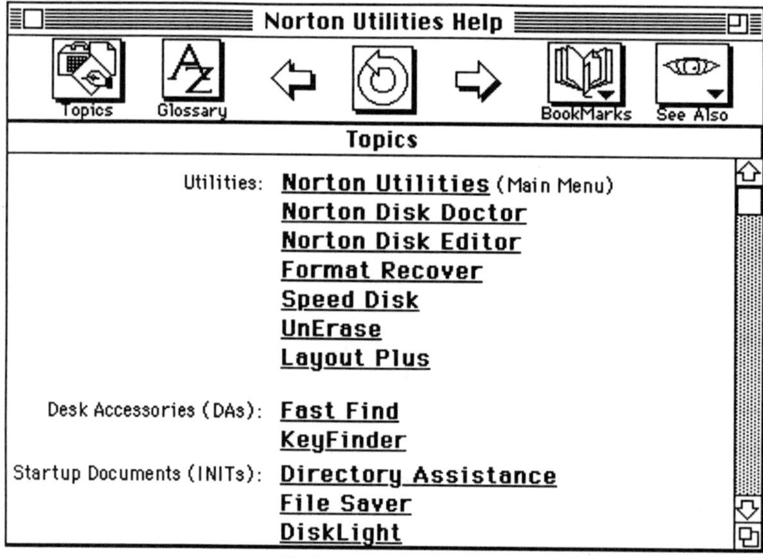

17-2 It has help files

The definition of the terms used in the manual to describe the operation of the software are shown in short form in Fig. 17-3. I chose a simple one for Fig. 17-4 just to keep it light and to see the use of graphics in the help files. The differences between ASCII text files and Mac text/graphics files makes reading them fun. The file sizes also make these types of files storage space intensive. Without all of the pretty pictures to make things easier and more fun, the file would be less than 30 percent of its current size.

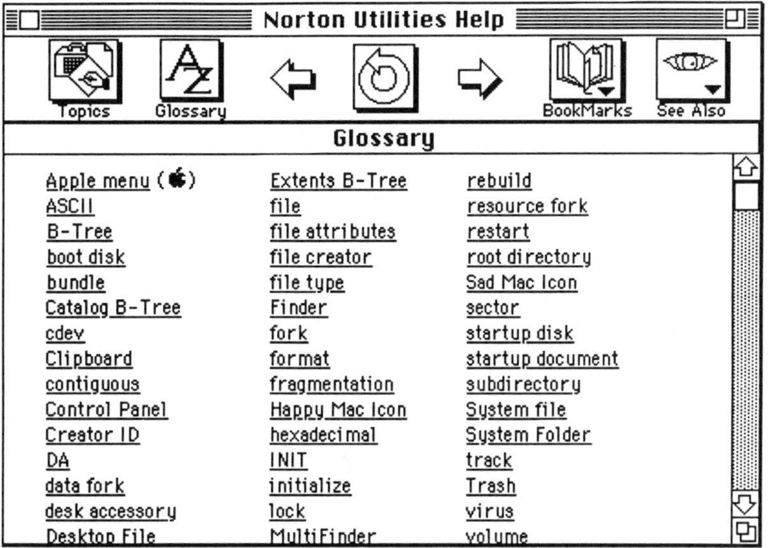

17-3 The glossary

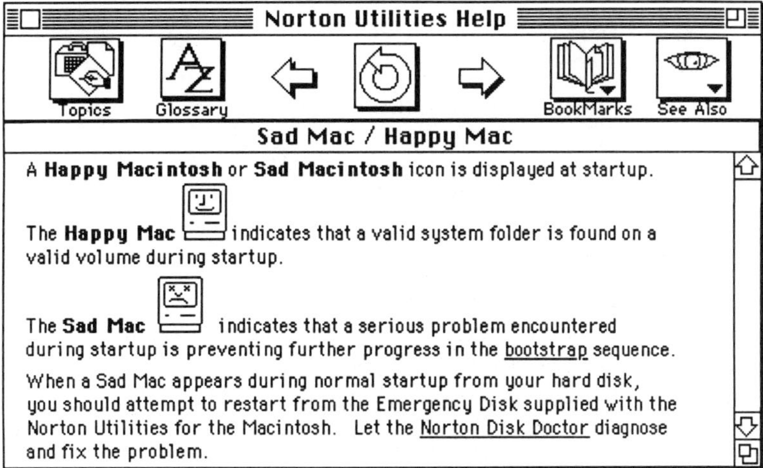

17-4 Two terms defined

FileSaver

The FileSaver icon is the life preserver. It's the one with the stripes on the diagonal if you happen to have AutoSave II installed, too. FileSaver's purpose in life is to make a file that is an index to your hard disks. This file is stored in a low traffic location, so it has maximum survivability. It also is the file that Format Recover and Quick UnErase use to assist their operations. These Utilities will work well without the FileSaver information; however, they will work faster and the probability of a greater recovery percentage is on the side of their being able to access the FileSaver file.

Concentrate your attention on the center portion of the screen image in Fig. 17-5. The button for Save Format Recover and UnErase info? should always be on. It will take up a limited amount of disk space. It also will delay your shutdown just a few seconds while it does an update of the file information. In return, it will have the data needed by those other utilities.

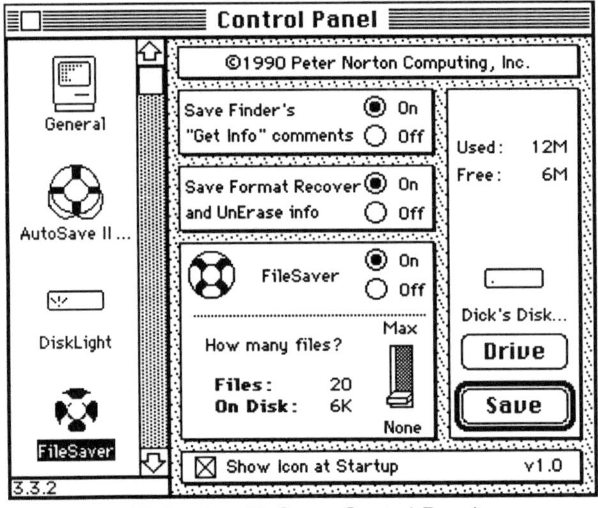

17-5 The FileSaver Control Panel

The setting for the button in the next section down is up to you. If you can afford to lose information, then leave it off. If there are novice users on the system, critical data is stored on the disk, it's the summer thunderstorm season when the power isn't as reliable as usual, etc., it too should be on. The amount of disk space required to keep track of the deleted files is proportional to the number of files you want saved. This saving process isn't anything like the save done by an application program or Auto-Save II. Those saves write the current information to an active file on your disk. FileSaver saves deleted files until it runs out of space or you need its space for active files.

As more files are added to its log, FileSaver deletes the older ones. It releases the space used by those files back to the system. When this happens, the recovery potential for these files drops rapidly. Until FileSaver releases the space, the potential for recovery of a deleted file in its log is excellent. Check it out with the UnErase Utility. The right-hand column displays the utility's assessment of the recoverability of the deleted files. Files that have just been deleted (as in less than a few minutes ago) and those that still are under FileSaver's protection will display "excellent" as the prognosis for recovery. When you see the word "poor" for a prognosis, you also might see a file size of zero bytes, too.

Unless you have unlimited disk space, you will overwrite deleted files at some point in time. It is much smarter to use backup files to recover accidentally deleted files than it is to attempt to provide unlimited disk space. Using backups to recover files means that you are going to have to keep your backups current. While this is viewed by some as nonproductive time, it takes only one serious problem to convert even the most hard-core opponent of backups.

If you back up each evening just before shutting the system down, you can keep a small FileSaver for a single day's work. If you don't back up each day, it might be wise to make the FileSaver file a little larger. Because this is an adjustment you can make, it will take a few days or weeks of experimentation to get the best size. Once this is done, it shouldn't be necessary to change things until there is a significant change in the way you use your computer. When that time comes, you will have to go through the process again. It should be easier and quicker because this will be a repeat rather than an initial adjustment.

Norton Disk Doctor

Perhaps the last doctor to make house calls, Norton's Disk Doctor (Fig. 17-6) is ready any time you need it. It takes a few minutes to let the Doctor check your system, but it's well worth

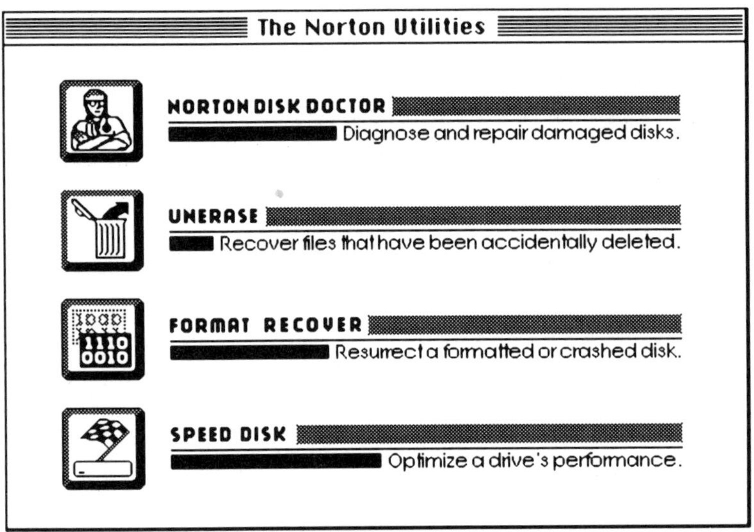

17-6 The Norton Utilities Selection screen

the time. While you get a cup of coffee, the Doctor can check out everything. No need to worry about things happening while you are away from your system. When there's a problem, the Doctor will open a dialog box for consultation with a recommendation and then await your decision. Under most circumstances, take the Doctor's advice.

There might be a few cases where expert users will have made changes that Disk Doctor assumes are errors but that should not be corrected. In these cases, just skip the repair procedure.

Don't let the fact that only six icons are displayed (Fig. 17-7) lead you to believe that only six tests are being conducted. A number of different tests are conducted while each of the icons is active. The exact number isn't given, but I've been told that the total is near 100 different things that are checked as part of the Disk Doctor Utility.

It is possible for a problem to escape the Disk Doctor. It is unlikely that such a problem will cause you much of a problem over time. Viruses and rouge programs are not the specialty of Disk Doctor. These types of programs will not be detected or corrected by Disk Doctor. The only time Disk Doctor might discover that such a program is active is when it has damaged the types of things that Disk Doctor is designed to detect and correct.

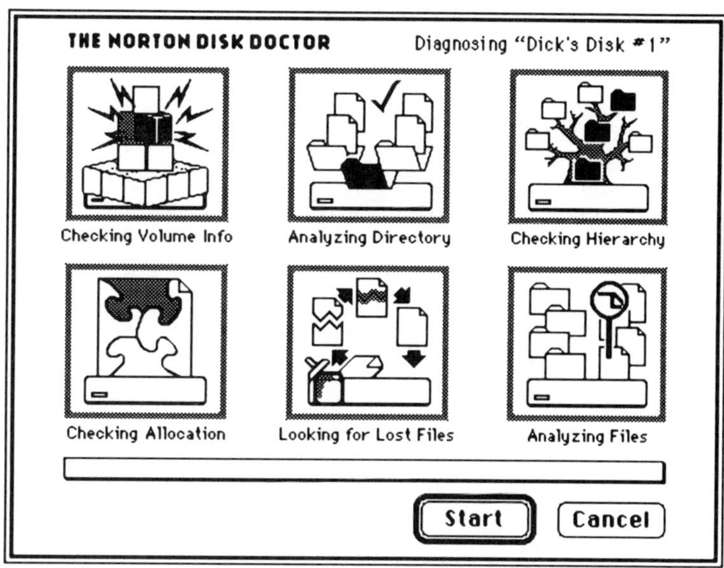

17-7 The Disk Doctor screen

Running the Disk Doctor can provide a few surprises. As seen in the report shown in Fig. 17-8, not everything was in order. Note the time of the report (4:01 P.M.) and the time the disk was last initialized (2:17 P.M.). Both happened on the same day (January 1, 1991). There are a number of possibilities for this

```
Norton Disk Doctor
Report for "Dick's Disk #1"
Tuesday, January 1, 1991 4:01 PM

System  Information:
Machine Name:
Macintosh Plus, 4 Megabytes of RAM

System Area Status:
The Boot Blocks check out OK and indicate that this is a bootable disk.
The Volume Information Block is OK.
There were some problems with the Directory.  These problems have been
fixed.

Disk  Statistics:
This is an HFS disk.
19,942,400 bytes total disk space.
8,417,280 bytes used by 113 files in 19 folders.
311,296 bytes used by the system area.
11,213,824 bytes available on the disk (10,951K free).
```

17-8 The Disk Doctor's report

17-8.   continued

Disk Technical Information:
This disk was initialized on Tuesday, January 1, 1991 2:17 PM
This disk was last modified on Tuesday, January 1, 1991 3:58 PM
There are 38,950 allocation blocks on this volume.
The Allocation Size is 1 block (512 bytes).
The volume bit map starts at sector #3.
The first sector represented in the volume bit map is #13.

File Status:
113 files were scanned.
77 had resource forks.

These files have valid bundle resources but their bundle bit was not set.
NDD has fixed this problem, but before the Finder will recognize the
changes, you must rebuild your disk's desktop file. See your manual if you
need help doing this.
Dick's Disk #1:MW II:Thesaurus:WF Large Thesaurus

These files have missing or damaged bundle resources and their bundle bit
was improperly set. NDD has fixed this problem, but before the Finder
will see the changes, you must rebuild your desktop file. See your manual
for more information.

Dick's Disk #1:MW II:Claris Translators:AppleWorks GS
Dick's Disk #1:MW II:Claris Translators:Microsoft Works 1.1
Dick's Disk #1:MW II:Claris Translators:TIFF
Dick's Disk #1:Utilities Folder:101-KEYS DA Remover

System Folder Details:
The active System files on this disk are:
Dick's Disk #1:System Folder:System   (version 6.0.4)
Dick's Disk #1:System Folder:Finder   (version 6.1.4)
Dick's Disk #1:System Folder:MultiFinder   (version 6.0.4)

The active INITs and cdevs on this disk are:
AutoSave II 1.11
Directory Assistance   (version 1.0)
DiskLight   (version 1.0)
Easy Access   (version 1.0.1)
FileSaver   (version 1.0)
General   (version 3.3.2)
Keyboard   (version 3.3.1)
MasterStrokes   (.MasterStrokes)
Mouse   (version 3.3.1)
Screenshot™   (version 60)
Sound   (version 3.3.1)

Summary:
The drive appears to be in working order. Frequent backups will insure the
integrity of your data.

type of a report so soon after an initialization. If these programs were returned to the disk via a backup copy, then the problems might have existed before the initialization. If they were loaded from locked diskettes that came from the developer, then there might be a problem with the system.

When problems have been repaired by Disk Doctor, it also reminds you to take any other actions needed to completely resolve the problem. Do not take this disk or its organization as being typical. It has been cleared of almost everything but the utility programs and a word processor program. One or two of the active INITs have not been installed. These are the virus detectors.

This utility will run from your mounted hard disk. Speed Disk, the other utility necessary for good performance, will not. To keep things simple, you might want to build a startup diskette that will hold the utilities and the necessary System and Finder Files to get everything done in an orderly manner. Doing it this way also will reduce the chances that something will be omitted. Another advantage of having everything on a single diskette is that you will not be interrupting the process. Getting half way through is only a little better than not running the utilities at all.

UnErase

It doesn't have a hole in it, but UnErase (Fig. 17-9) is a true life saver. The DOS version of this program started Peter Norton on his career many years ago. In the less than ten years since the first version appeared, things have changed to the point that it would be almost impossible for the original version of that utility to work. This also is why there have been updates to the program almost yearly. The only person I know who will never have a need for this program is someone who never uses a computer. Network managers can do a good job of protecting things and backups will replace a good percentage of what was lost. Only UnErase or a similar utility will get back what you did but lost through a mistake.

UnErase also can recover all or a portion of the information that has been left on diskettes that have been used previously and not been reinitialized. For this reason, be sure you either protect your diskettes or reformat them when you are done. A number of

17-9 Beginning to UnErase

embarrassing incidents have happened over the years because the sending user forgot that the delete command doesn't really erase the entire file. Reformatting doesn't take all that much time and the benefits are well worth the effort.

A magnet also will completely erase information from a diskette. The problem with using this method is that it also erases the media descriptor information on the diskette. If this information, which is in the first sector of the diskette, is missing, your system will not be able to read the diskette correctly. One of the problems that occurs with this type of error is that it usually isn't discovered when you attempt to initialize the diskette. This means that you also can use the diskette for backups, which you won't be able to read and for copies, which you might not be able to read. Doing a bit copy of a good diskette to a damaged diskette might overcome the problem.

UnErase (Fig. 17-10) can work because, when you delete, trash, or otherwise dispose of a file, all of the information that is the file is not immediately destroyed. In essence, the only thing that is lost is the listing for the file as an active file. This listing tells the system that all of the space that was being used by the file is now free for use. Just because the space is available doesn't mean that it will be used by the next write operation.

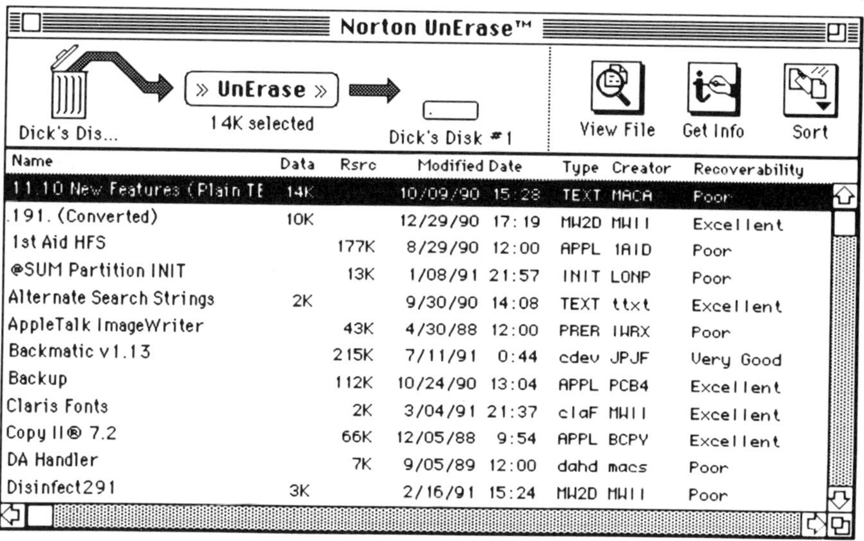

17-10 The UnErase Selection screen

The system works more efficiently when all of a file's data is in contiguous sectors, that there are no gaps in the information from first to last sector. However, gaps do occur. That condition is known as fragmenting. Fragmented files will run without error; they just take a bit longer to load or launch. Unfragmented files also are easier to unerase.

With FileSaver active and with regular doses of Disk Doctor and Speed Disk, you shouldn't have any trouble recovering any file that gets deleted accidently. UnErase will recover it almost instantly if you use the utility immediately after you delete the file. Using Disk Doctor and Speed Disk on a regular basis also will keep you confident that your system is fully functional and operating at maximum efficiency. It also means that you are being careful and might never really need UnErase. Don't feel bad if this is the case. Remember that the purpose of many of these utilities is to help you after things have gone wrong. The rest of them are to help you keep things from going wrong.

Format Recover

All might not be lost even if the worst happens. Depending on what's happened and what preparations were made ahead of time, it really might only be a minor inconvenience. It is more difficult to accidentally reformat, or reinitialize, a Mac hard disk than it is to make the same mistake in the DOS world. Erase Hard Disk is on the Special Menu and is between commands that you might use regularly.

If you hit the erase hard disk box and that operation begins, there are only a few choices available. You can cry a lot. You might get vicious and destroy the system. Another possibility is to shut the power off and contemplate what other options are available. You also could let things progress normally and, after the disk has been erased, you can use Format Recover (Fig. 17-11) to get everything back in working order.

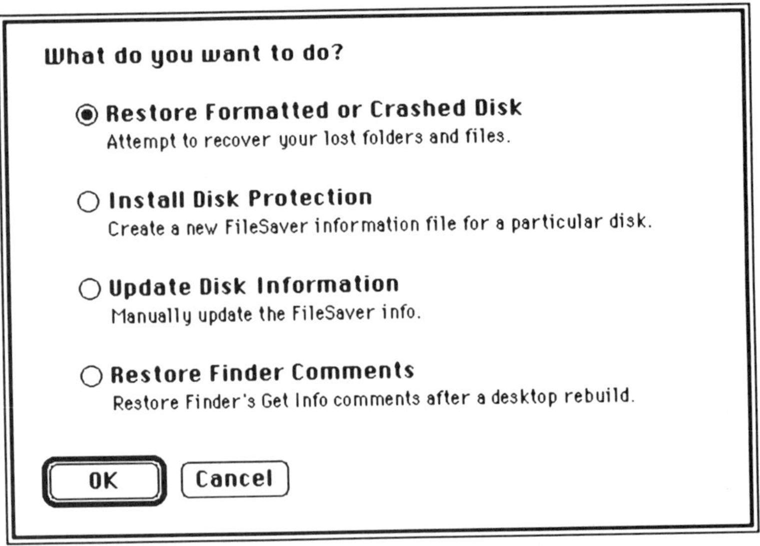

17-11   Format Recover's first screen

I'm making some assumptions as I go along here. One is that you really are interested in being an effective user. Another is that data loss concerns you and you are interested in ways to prevent it. You also are interested in keeping data loss to a minimum if you can't prevent it completely.

Speed Disk

Speed Disk is more of a partial description of what happens after you use this Utility than a true name. It really is a disk optimizer utility. There are a number of pieces of important information available on the screen (Fig. 17-12). This illustration was made after Speed Disk had run its course. The black area of the screen indicates the disk space that contains information. The white space is the free space on the disk. The magnifying glass moves in response to mouse movement. The windows in the bottom left side provide the information. In this illustration, the last filled sector is 26,431. The file there is a part of the Desktop. The next window over doesn't reflect this because Speed Disk cannot run from your hard disk. It must be run from a floppy.

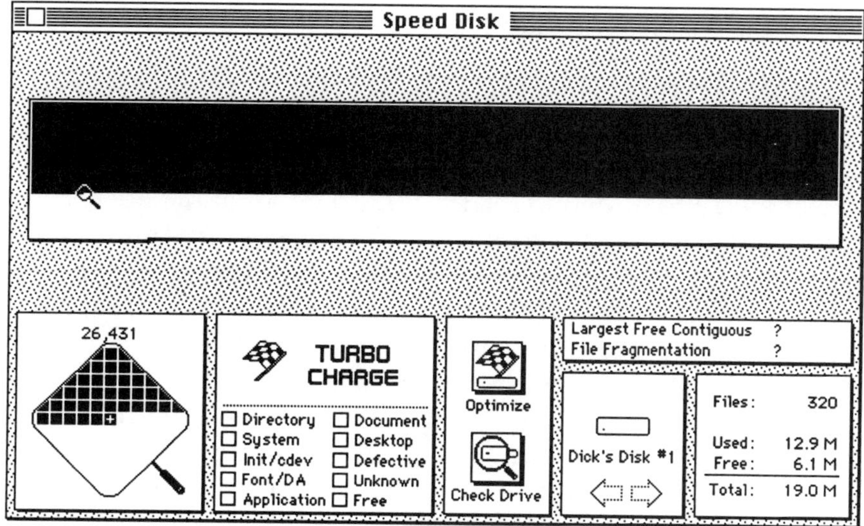

17-12 The Speed Disk screen

During the course of normal operations, the information stored in the various files on your disks gets changed. Some of these changes add length to the file, while others shorten it. Deleting files leaves gaps in the stream of sectors. These gaps get used for file storage over time. The problem with using these gaps is that they are seldom the correct length for the new file. The remaining space will be used later for another piece of a different file, perhaps one that wouldn't fit in an earlier gap on the disk.

The system software can, and does, keep track of all of these file segments. As you call for the files, the heads of the disk drive move to the proper location and read the data. If the entire file isn't at that location, the system then tells the heads where to find the next portion of the information. Each wait for a new location and each move costs time. On a one time basis, this time loss isn't significant. If you add the loss to all of the other similar losses over a day or a week's time, they can become worthy of notice. The other factor involved is the wear and tear on the drive mechanism. Having to bounce back and forth between locations to read the disconnected sectors of a file can cause the drive to fail sooner.

One way to reduce wear and tear, along with keeping files together, is to make it a practice to run a series of utilities at the beginning or end of each day. It also might make sense to run part of the series at night, just before shut down and backup. You then can run the remaining programs when you restart the system the next morning. The advantage to this scheme is to make it easier to back up your work that evening and to ensure that the system is in good working order before you start the next day.

If I were to develop such a plan, I'd do all of the housekeeping in the evening and all of the testing in the morning. Speed Disk and the backup software would run after all of the files, folders, and volumes were closed for the night. I also would make a quick check of the files being protected by FileSaver and eliminate any I was sure wouldn't be needed again.

The next morning, I'd run Disk Doctor's full set of utilities before opening the first application for business. This plan will cost me less than 30 minutes each day, not counting the time to make backups, which I easily can justify. Saving that time now only to spend it doing a full-blown recovery of a hard disk is not an economy that is justifiable.

One of the possible difficulties that occurs when a hard disk is not kept in reasonable order is that the system can become confused and record that the same space is being used by two files. These might be text or ASCII files that can be read from the screen during the recovery operation. They also can be compiled application program files, which will make it almost impossible to determine which sector comes next in which file. I have found that it is much easier to delete both of the programs and to reload them. It takes less time and I don't get nearly as frustrated.

The rub comes when the problem file is neither a text nor a compiled application. These usually are the data files written by application programs in some type of compressed form or graphics files. When this happens, recovery is still possible. It will just take longer and might not be as successful. Good operating procedures or safe hex can reduce these types of problems to a minimum.

Norton Disk Editor

Warning: This utility is powerful. You can do at least as much damage through misuse as you can good through proper use. The Norton Disk Editor can display every sector of every disk you can get your system to read. This also means that it can make changes to every sector of every disk read. This is an excellent feature and a loose cannon all rolled into one. When you have problems, you can fix them. If you're not careful, you can destroy everything, including access to the disk. If you need this utility, use it. Just be smart and don't abuse it. There are safety measures built into the program, but they are not able to keep you from doing irrecoverable damage. This is because it is these types of changes that are sometimes necessary to correct problems caused by other incidents.

This is the beginning. Figure 17-13 displays sector zero. As you can see, this is the first sector of a bootable disk. If the information in this sector isn't correct, your system will not be able to read any of the other information stored on the disk. The same holds true for the boot sector of a diskette. The initial contact between the system and the disk must be correct or it will

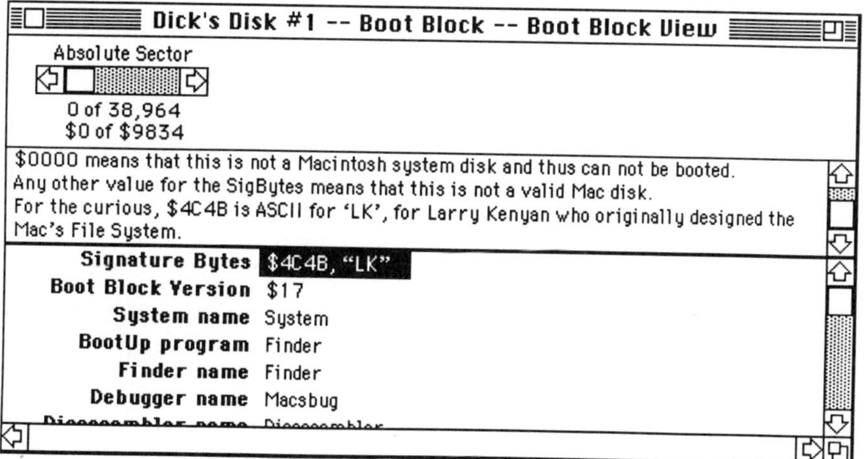

17-13 The boot block is where it begins

not continue. If this sector is bad, the whole thing crashes. It is possible to view this area in hex mode so that changes can be made. Be sure you know what you are doing before making any changes here.

When you start using the Disk Edit program, remember that any changes you make will be permanent. Disk Edit writes directly to the disk and overwrites the information that was there. In cases where this information was in error, you are correcting a problem. In a case where the correct data is changed, you can cause yourself many hours of work just trying to get back to where you were. Figure 17-14 illustrates a listing of folders. Toward the bottom, you can see the beginning of the applications programs listing. The alphabetical listing of each of the sections isn't something I've done to make things easy for you. This is the way that Disk Edit presents its listings.

Name	Data	Resource	Type	Creator	Modified
☐ Dick's Disk #1					
🗀 HyperCard	–	–	6 files		1/01/91
🗀 MacTools® Deluxe Folder	–	–	8 files		1/01/91
🗀 MW II	–	–	18 files		1/05/91
🗀 Norton Utilities	–	–	4 files		1/01/91
🗀 Search String Sets	–	–	2 files		11/08/90
🗀 System Folder	–	–	39 files		1/04/91
🗀 Template Folder	–	–	6 files		6/30/89
🗀 Utilities Folder	–	–	3 files		1/01/91
Extractor	30,468		APPL	EXTC	8/02/90
Minor•Repairs	6,402		APPL	MRp1	8/29/90
Virex® 2.81	120,928		APPL	VIRy	1/04/91

17-14 Looking at the folders with Disk Edit

Look at the left portion of the listing in Fig. 17-15. Like the previous folder listing, you are given more than just the file/folder name while in Disk Edit. Each piece of information shown provides you with a better idea of what the file is all about and what to expect when you actually go in and begin to look around.

The top of the screen (Fig. 17-16) provides the information on what is being displayed in the lower portion. Changes made

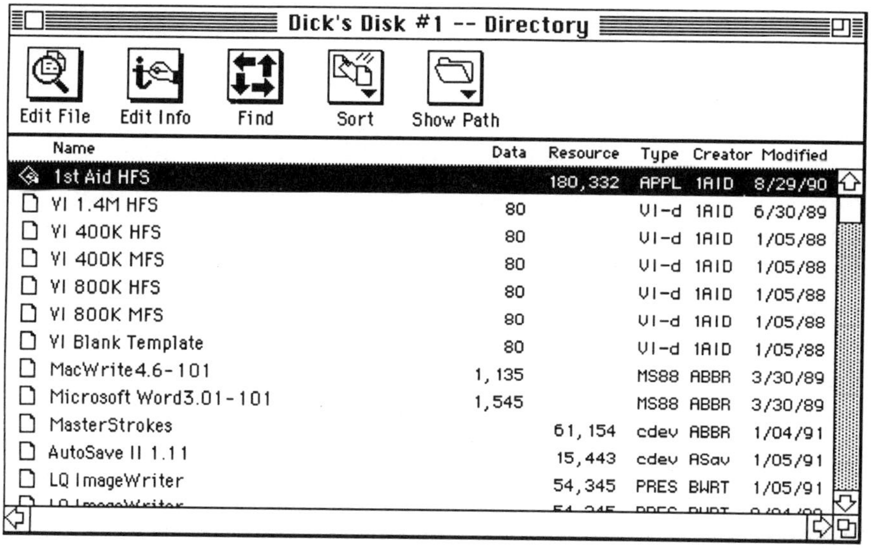

17-15   Checking out the documents

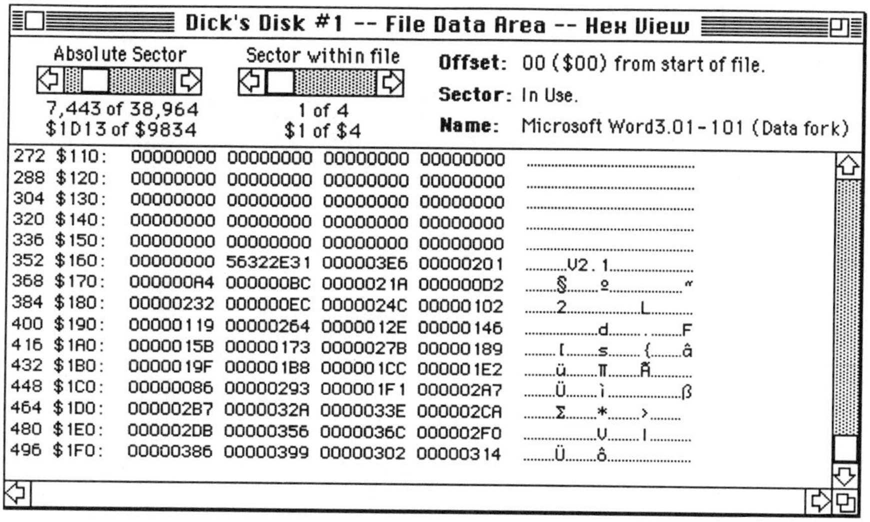

17-16   A file in Hex View

on the left side must be valid hex values, while changes made on the right side are ASCII characters. You normally can not enter all of the ASCII values from the keyboard as keystrokes. This is where being able to enter hex values becomes important. It also is important to enter the correct value. If your table of values gets worn or hard to read be sure to replace it. You should be keeping it next to your keyboard while editing at this level. A good table will have the decimal values, the hex values, and the keyboard characters or combination keypress notations. There are a total of FFh or 255d values. Make sure you are using the correct one.

The cursor is visible in Fig. 17-17, which makes it easy to see which portion of the screen is active for editing. The underline character is the indicator. It's in the text portion of the screen. This is why the hex value 69h is in reverse video. When the situation is reversed, the underline would be under a single hex value and the reverse video block would occupy a single space in the text portion of the screen.

```
╔══════════ Dick's Disk #1 -- File Data Area -- Hex View ══════════╗

   Absolute Sector        Sector within file     Offset:  24,064 ($5E00) from start of file.
 ◁▒▒▒▒[  ]▒▒▒▒▷         ◁[ ]▒▒▒▒▒▒▒▷          Sector:  In Use.
   23,355 of 38,964         48 of 2001         Name:    CPS-1544512731 (Data fork)
   $5B3B of $9834           $30 of $7D1

000 $000:  69736B73 2028652E 672E2C20 696E4855    isks (e.g., inHU
016 $010:  6E697665 72736974 79206C61 62732077    niversity labs w
032 $020:  69746820 666C6F70 70792D6F 6E6C7920    ith floppy-only
048 $030:  4D616373 292E2054 68652049 4E495420    Macs). The INIT
064 $040:  646F6573 206E6F74 20696E74 65726665    does not interfe
080 $050:  72652077 69746849 74686520 6E6F726D    re with the norm
096 $060:  616C206F 70657261 74696F6E 206F6620    al operation of
112 $070:  44697369 6E666563 74616E74 206F7220    Disinfectant or
128 $080:  6F746865 7220616E 74692D76 6972616C    other anti-viral
144 $090:  20617070 6C696361 74696F6E 732C206F     applications, o
160 $0A0:  72467769 74682070 726F6772 616D6D69    rFwith programmi
176 $0B0:  6E672065 6E766972 6F6E6D65 6E74732C    ng environments,
192 $0C0:  20696E73 74616C6C 65722061 70706C69     installer appli
208 $0D0:  63617469 6F6E732C 206F7220 6F746865    cations, or othe
```

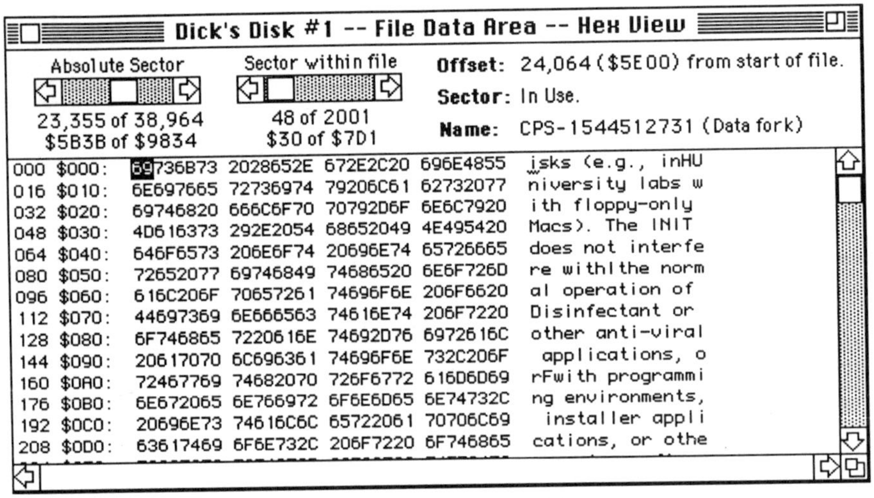

17-17 A text file in Hex View

Changes made in either side cause the changed characters on both sides to be highlighted. This is a reminder that you have changed things. It also makes it easier for you to review your work a few times before making it permanent. Disk Edit will not allow you to leave this screen until you make a decision on any changes you have made. You can either save them (allow them to be written to disk) or discarded (no changes made to existing data).

Not being able to leave the screen before making a decision is a safety measure. Disk Edit doesn't want you to forget that you have made changes and doesn't want the changes getting lost in your rush to get everything up and running right. There also is a practical side to having your decision before moving on. The changes are in RAM and on the screen only until decision time. The overhead necessary to keep track of your changes through multiple screens would eat RAM faster than any other situation I could imagine. A crash during this type of operation could create even more problems than you are currently facing.

Start at the beginning, go slowly, check your work carefully, and stop either at the end or earlier (if you are making more mistakes than you are correcting). Repair and recovery operations are not instant fixes. Even when these utilities are able to perform the necessary corrective tasks automatically, it takes time. When you have to do them manually, it will take much longer. Be prepared for it and don't get frustrated. If it's absolutely necessary, you can write every byte to a hard disk. Hopefully, you will never face a situation where that's necessary.

Layout Plus

Layout Plus does nothing for you that you can't do for yourself. Why consider using the utility then? For one thing, Layout Plus can do the same work easier and quicker than you can. Another plus for the utility is that it always does the same thing the same way. You don't have to remember a thing about the procedure. It replaces and enhances the way your screens are formatted. I have a problem from time to time of dumping one icon into a folder on top of an existing icon. As long as I remember to check that folder out before I quit, I usually uncover the first icon.

There have been times when I have forgotten to do this and then couldn't find a file. It's not a major disaster, but it can be a major frustration. (I'd show you the Layout Plus screen, but my little system didn't have enough memory from both the utility and the screen grabber to be active at the same time. This is going to be one of those cases where I'm going to have to refer you to the manual so you can see the illustration there. You'll find it on page 109 in your software manual. It's at the top of the page, so you shouldn't be able to miss it.)

Don't be satisfied with a layout that is almost what you want. Launch Layout Plus as often as necessary or until you get everything the way you want it. I like seeing the filenames, so I use small icons in my display. This serves two purposes. First, I still can get all of the files in any one folder compressed onto one screen. No panning is required. Second, it is a continuous reminder that I'm on a different system. The CADD packages that I use are on a DOS-based system and everything there is text.

Fast Find

Nobody likes to lose things. Large hard disks are great places to hide them. Any time there are more files on the disk than can be comfortably displayed on a single screen, things will get lost. Trying to find them can consume time, like some people consume chocolate.

The Hierarchical File System (HFS) makes it easier to do logical searches. It also means that every path must be traced to its end before you can be sure that what you're looking for isn't there. Using Fast Find can reduce search time to almost nothing. This can be more important when there are large drives to be searched. One 40Mb drive can be searched in relatively short order. A few hundred megabytes on a number of drives takes time.

The screen illustrated in Fig. 17-18 shows you the way to get a handle on your files. By entering at least a small portion of the filename in the Search For block, you can let Fast Find do the hard part of looking. I used micro as a key word because it was bound to find a number of files with that as the first part of the filename.

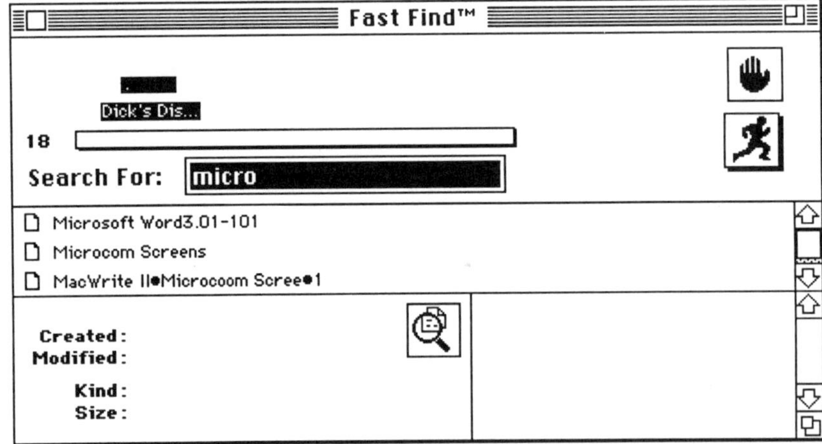

17-18   The Fast Find screen

According to the information provided by Fast Find (Fig. 17-19), there are 18 files on my hard disk with micro as the first part of the filename. When one of them is selected, the bottom left portion of the screen provides the details about the file itself, while the bottom right portion displays the full path to the file. I didn't try to time the search because it was finished before I could check my watch.

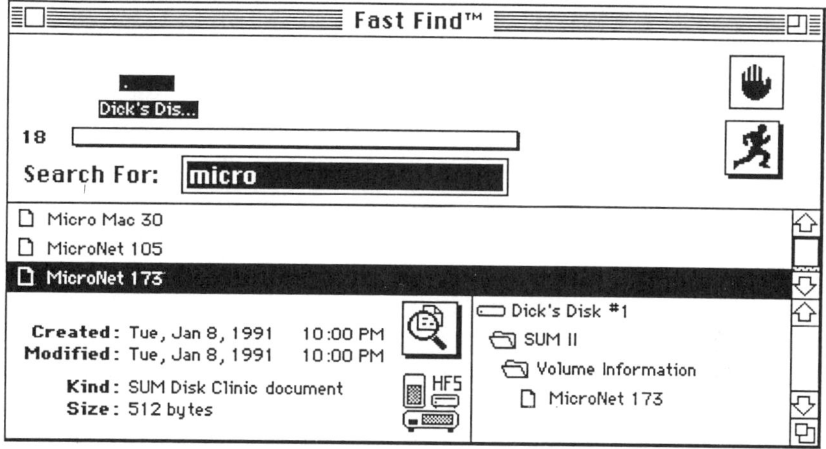

17-19 Fast Find after the search

Once you've selected the file you think is the one you're looking for, you can go further. Fast Find will allow you to view the first 32K of the file. This is done without launching the creator application. Be warned that the information won't look exactly like it does when you view it from within the creator.

Under most circumstances, a less than ideal display of the information should be enough to allow you to confirm that you have found the proper file. Now that you have the file, you don't have to give it up to really use it. Fast Find provides a means for moving it to your Desktop. Finder has the means to return it to its original location. You can do what must be done while the file is in the Desktop and then return it to its proper location. You also should make a note of where you found it, so you don't have to use the same method to relocate it.

KeyFinder

When this utility comes in the DOS version of the Norton Utilities, I will be happy. One of the problems that occurs when working with different typeface sets (as in desktop publishing) is that not every set places the same character in the same place. In one typeface, you might see a "smiley face" when you press the Option–E combination. If you change typefaces, this same combination keypress might result in an *e* with an umlaut or a dagger being displayed. The dagger could come from a number of typeface possibilities.

Dingbats is all symbols. There is a different symbol for each of the ASCII characters common to your regular keyboard. My problem was that, when the software arrived, there was no translation table enclosed. Before I could even start trying to use it, I had to write my own translation table. With KeyFinder that would have been unnecessary and I could have pulled it up almost any time I needed help.

Another use for the KeyFinder screen is getting the proper combination keypress to use things like the registered trademark or the copyright symbol (Fig. 17-20).

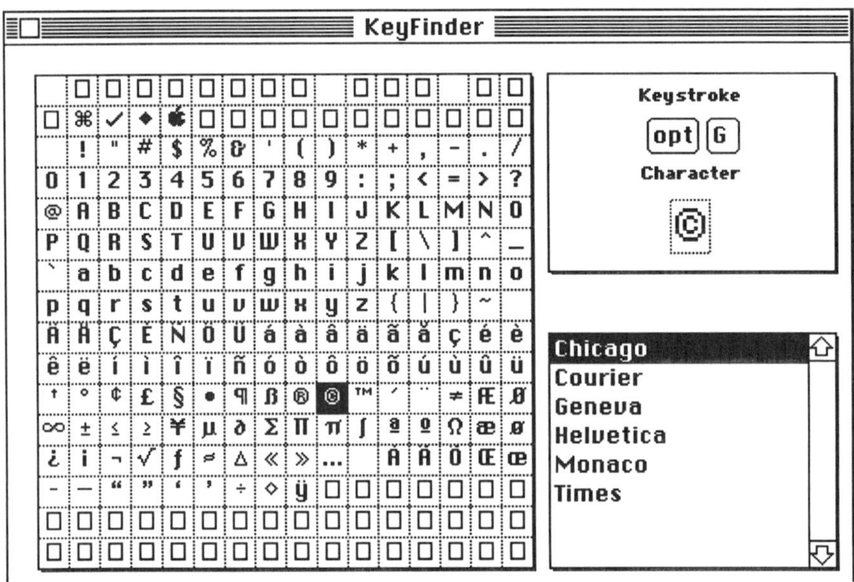

17-20 KeyFinder and the copyright symbol

Figures 17-20 and 17-21 illustrate one method of using Key-Finder. You use the mouse to highlight the character you want to enter into your document and the necessary keypress combination is displayed. The reverse operation also is possible. You can

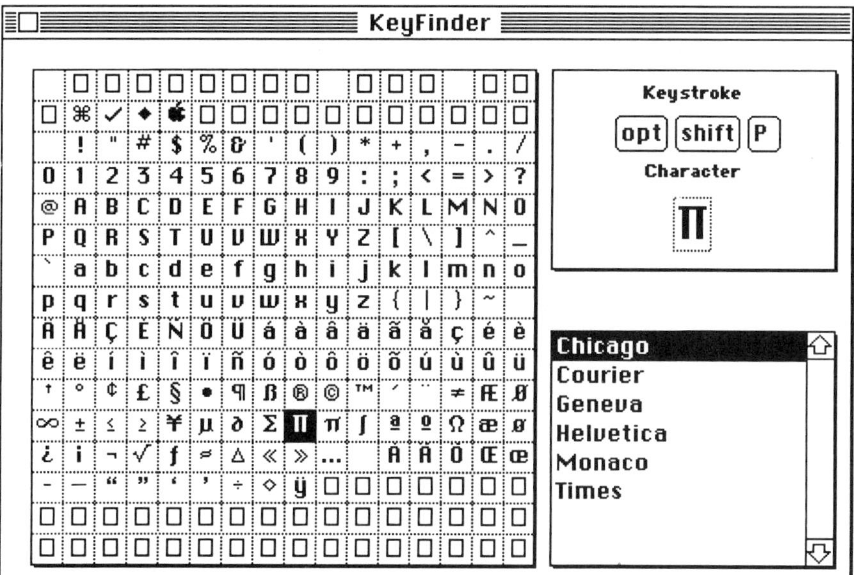

17-21 KeyFinder and a different symbol

enter a combination and the utility will highlight the character that should result.

Desktop publishers should enjoy having this little gem waiting in the wings. Each typeface will have some variations. By using KeyFinder during the creation process, it should not be necessary to place blanks or dummy characters in any location where the font file provides the proper character. Just be sure you have your fingers limbered up. Some of the symbols will require a three-finger keypress.

Directory Assistance

Like many of the other Norton Utilities, Directory Assistance isn't a replacement program; it is a compliment. Also, like many of the other utilities, it can replace a standard program. When using Open, Save, or Save As under the File menu, there are a few preset limitations with the standard program. Directory Assistance tries to provide a way to eliminate many of the limitations.

The enhancements are provided to make your life easier. While you're in an application, you can open and close files, as well as folders, on any of the volumes that are mounted. You might be wondering if you can delete them, get into cleanup even farther and delete entire groups of files and folders, or change the listing setup. With the standard program, the options are limited. Clicking the View button will open a whole new world of options to you. Neither Finder nor MultiFinder can provide these features. Directory Assistance provides most of them. If it provided all of them in this first release, there wouldn't be any way to improve the software. There also would be a steep learning curve for this complex piece of software. I suspect that there would be a much higher price tag on the package. In its present form, there is all the power that most users can cope with and just enough to ensure that power-hungry users will be waiting with baited breath for the next release.

Mastering packages like these utility programs isn't the easiest thing in the world. They can rank close to the top of the most difficult list if you do not take time out to read the manual between play sessions. (I call them play because I never make time to search out hidden features or try new things with a utility package while I'm trying to get something else done.)

To get to know a package, I have to work with it. This means hours of nothing but trying to do things. Things that work are fun, but those that don't drive me to the book. During the search for one thing, I'm often distracted by finding some other feature I don't need immediately but would like to know more about. This isn't always a logical means of learning about a programs features. Using a logical approach is much more efficient and will allow you to learn more in less time. I've got to learn how to do that just as soon as I get some time.

One of the things I love and hate about the Delete command is that it has safeties built into it. It will let you delete any file that is not otherwise protected. It will let me delete folders too. However, they must be empty folders. To prove its point, when you use the delete command in Directory Assistance, the files in the folder you are attempting to delete will be displayed. Even if you are sure that you want the files to go where you were attempting to send the folder, you will have to arrange separate transportation. The files in a folder, like the files in a subdirectory, must be deleted or moved out of the folder or subdirectory before you can delete the folder or subdirectory.

This type of safety net is important. When I'm at work on a project, I will sometimes start trashing things without thinking about the consequences to get more storage space. (I should compress the files and place them on floppies or another form of media storage.) After all of the files are gone that I think I can live without, I sometimes will look at the subdirectories. Any of them that I think I can live without are subject to getting tossed into the bit bucket.

To date, I've only done that sort of thing once when I couldn't recover a few of the files that I later discovered held some important information. In one case, I didn't even have a hardcopy backup. (I will not repeat here what I said then.) Since then, I have been a firm believer in backups. This is one of the reasons that I stress them so often. I'd hate to think that there will be other grown persons crying because they didn't have a second copy of something. Directory Assistance has a neat little feature in it that can help you keep your eyes dry. The Duplicate feature makes a copy of any file and automatically names it Copy of. . . .

You also will find another Get Info type of screen buried in Directory Assistance. It is much different from the standard screen and will give you another look at an image of the man responsible for all of these utilities. (Peter might have moved on to bigger and better things, but I doubt that you will go long before you hear about him again. Even if he does take an extended vacation, the team of people that he assembled still is in place and working hard to make the utilities better and more mistake-proof.)

The last of the features I must mention is the ability to order the display in Directory Assistance. The display can be set to display by name, date, or size, with the folders listed first or last. This ability can save time when you start searching. If you reorder the files by date, the last ones you created should come to the top of the listing. If you were looking for a file that was created three days ago and only one is listed, that should be the file; however, it might not be because there are files that are not displayed while you are in an application. All of the files that can be opened while you are in that application will display but no others. Therefore, if you used the open application to create the file, you did it three days ago, and there is only one file with that creation date, there is a good chance that the file you want is the file displayed.

If it isn't, you might try checking some of your other disk-ettes and volumes. I try to keep similar files grouped, but I don't always succeed. Come housecleaning time, I find all sorts of things in the dusty corners of the system. The system forgets less than I do, so we get along. I try to be creative and it keeps me logical. There's a balance there someplace, but I haven't found it yet. I'll keep looking, though. It might be in one of those still-to-be-cleaned corners.

DiskLight

Under many circumstances, it doesn't make a lot of difference whether or not you know when your system is doing a disk read or write. It could make a difference if your system is unprotected and there were disk operations going on at times when you wouldn't expect them. Trojan horse programs do it all the time. While your attention should be directed toward the screen, it is doing dirty business to your disks.

With the DiskLight utility active, you will see an indication of every disk related activity on your screen. The exact location of the indicator is your choice, although it is somewhat limited by the programmers. You also will notice in Fig. 17-22 that the indication is different for hard disk read/write operations. When the read/write operation is to a diskette, the icon changes to the

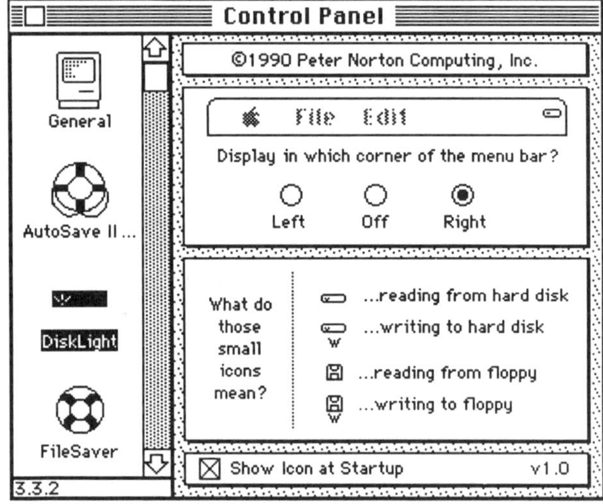

17-22   DiskLight's Control Panel

outline of a diskette. The hard disk icon looks like an external hard disk, if you use your imagination, so it should be easy to differentiate the two.

I agree that this isn't one of those utilities that I'd kill for, but I think you will agree that it makes a nice addition to this package. Not installing and using it will not crash your system nor will it make it any easier to perform recovery operations when the crash does come. However, it can serve as a reminder that read/write operations are being performed. That should be enough to keep you alert to unusual happenings.

If your hard disk is placed so that you are unable to see the light at a casual glance, then this utility can become more important. My other system is sitting on the floor under my desk. It, too, has a hard drive, so I don't need to get to the diskette drives very often. This being the case, to protect it as much as possible, I have it pushed back away from where it might get damaged by free swinging feet, small children seeing the lights and wanting to play with the buttons, as well as the various electromechanical floor cleaning devices that visit the immediate vicinity.

Appendix

Following is a list of the developers that have contributed the products showcased in this book. All of them will sell direct. Most of them also market their products through distributors and retail outlets.

After you have reviewed all of the products in this book, you might want to check out the local users group or one of the bulletin board services. The users in either location will be more than happy to assist you in making your decisions. It will be almost impossible for you to get a set of utilities that have no overlap in the features. Hopefully, after reading this book, you will have a much better understanding of utilities and their purpose. I also would hope that you will be able to purchase those that will give you the most value for the buck.

Central Point Software, Inc.
15220 N.W. Greenbrier Parkway #200
Beaverton, OR 97006

Technical support: 8 A.M. to 5 P.M. (PST) on weekdays
(503) 690-8080

Fifth Generation Systems, Inc.
10049 N. Reiger Road
Baton Rouge, LA 70809

Technical support: (504) 291-9953
Sales: (800) 873-4384
Administrative: (504) 291-7221

Magic Software, Inc.
2239 Franklin Street
Bellevue, NE 68005

Questions: (800) 342-6243 or
         (402) 291-0670

Mainstay
5311B Derry Avenue
Agoura Hills, CA 91301

Questions: (818) 991-6540

Microcom Software
P.O. Box 51816
Durham, NC 27717

Questions: (919) 490-1277

John Norstad
Academic Computing and Network Services
Northwestern University
2129 Sheridan Road
Evanston, IL 60208

Electronic mail received at:

Internet	jln@casbah.acns.nwu.edu
Bitnet	jln@nuacc
AppleLink	a0173
America Online	JNORSTAD
Compuserve	76666,573

Jeffrey S. Shulman
P.O. Box 1218
Morgantown, WV 26507-1218

Questions: 6 P.M. to 9 P.M. (EST) on weekdays
11 A.M. to 9 P.M. (EST) on weekends
(304) 598-2090

Electronic mail received at:
AppleLink: KILROY
GEnie: KILROY
DELPHI: JEFFS
CompuServe: 76136,667
America Online: KILROY7

Symantec Corp.
10201 Torre Avenue
Cupertino, CA 95014

24-hour hotline: (408) 255-8744
Technical support: 8 A.M. to 12 P.M. and 1 P.M. to 5 P.M.
(PST) on weekdays
(408) 253-2167
Other calls: (408) 253-9600

Symantec Corp.
Peter Norton Computing Group
100 Wilshire Boulevard, Suite 900
Santa Monica, CA 90401

Customer service: (213) 319-2010
Technical support: (213) 319-2012

The following suppliers have proven to be reliable for me. They are listed in alphabetical order.

MacAvenue—A Division of CompuAdd Corporation
12303 Technology Boulevard
Austin, TX 78727
(800) 888-6221

MacConnection
14 Mill Street
Marlow, NH 03456
(800) 800-2222

MacWarehouse
P.O. Box 3013
1690 Oak Street
Lakewood, NJ 08701-3013
(800) 255-6227

Glossary

A

access time   The time it takes for the read/write head to move from wherever it is to the track that holds the beginning of the information you have requested. This time will vary depending on the relative locations of the two points in question.

analog   The term used to describe the form of information usually seen on clocks and speedometers. It displays changes by moving a pointer or with similar visible movement.

ASCII   The acronym for the American Standard Code for Information Interchange.

B

binary   Bi indicates two. Binary number system is a means of counting using only two numbers. In the case of microcomputers, these numbers are a one and a zero.

bit   A bit is a single binary digit. It is either a one or a zero.

boot   The term used to describe the activity involved in getting your computer up and running. It comes from the concept of pulling itself up by its own bootstraps. All of the instructions necessary for the computer to begin operation are contained within the computer either in the ROM or the disks.

byte   A byte is an ordered group of eight bits. Each byte has a specific meaning. All of the ASCII characters are contained in the first 255 bytes. The value of a byte of seven ones and a zero (0111 1111) is 255. The next byte of higher value is 256 (1000 0000).

C

cache   A portion of main memory (RAM) that is reserved for the temporary holding of blocks of input or output information. It usually is used to improve the speed of transfer between a slow device (the disk drive) and a fast device (RAM). By holding often used portions of disk files in RAM, it is possible to increase the efficiency of a system. Because the cache takes away from available RAM, it is best used only in systems that have at least enough RAM to run the largest anticipated application.

case sensitive   The ASCII code for each letter is different for the upper case and the lower case. If a search is case sensitive, then it has the ability to search for either case. When both cases are searched concurrently, the search is said to be case insensitive.

Cyclic Redundancy Check (CRC)   Another description of the "checksum" value, it is the value generated based on the value of all of the bytes written to each sector. It is written there immediately after the data bytes. When the computer returns to read that sector, the value of the bytes is calculated again. The old and new CRC values are then compared. If they are the same, the data is considered valid and is passed on. If there is a difference, an error message is generated.

cylinder   The collection of tracks at the same radius from the hub on both sides of all of the platters, hard or flexible.

D

data fork   One of the two forks in every Macintosh file. The information kept in this fork is subject to change. The other fork is the resource fork. A text document would normally have a long data fork with a zero length resource fork. The word processor that created it might be just the opposite.

default   Default values are those settings that are present when the computer or program beings operation. In most cases, these values can be changed. When they are, the new values or settings become the default values.

delete   To delete something normally means to erase or remove it. This meaning is modified in microcomputers because, when a file is deleted, not all of its parts are removed from the media at that time.

desk accessory   A small application program that is available almost all of the time that your system in powered up. The basic Desk Accessories are the Alarm Clock, Calculator, Chooser, Control Panel, Key Caps, and Scrapbook. Your hardware manual will give you many more details about all of these. Many of the utility programs described in this book also are Desk Accessories. Some of them are even replacements for the ones provided by Apple.

device driver   A special form of application program that manages the exchange of information between your computer and a peripheral device. Word Processor applications usually have a long list of printers that they support. This support comes in the form of device drivers supplied on the distribution diskette.

differential backup   A partial backup where only the files that have been changed since the last full backup are copied to the backup media. When the next differential backup is made it supersedes the previous differential backup because it also copies all of the files that have been changed since the last full backup was made.

digital   Each of the numbers from zero to nine is a digit. Microcomputers also are called digital computers because they work with the number units of the binary system. There are no fractions or parts of a number used in a digital computer. This does not mean that the results of its calculations cannot be fractional, real, or even imaginary.

download   The process of transferring a file from another system to your system, usually through the use of a modem. It also is possible to transfer files directly from system to system.

E

erase Erase and delete are sometimes used interchangeably. They also are used to differentiate between the way the delete function eliminates data from your computer and the way an eraser utility, like WipeDisk, works. Delete removes only the housekeeping information. This indicates to the system that that space now is available for use by other files. Erasing a disk usually involves overwriting all parts of it with a value, which effectively removes any possibility of recovery. In cases where government security is involved, the procedure is repeated a number of times and then read to ensure that the erase function was successful.

error message Messages that appear on the screen usually mean the user has made a mistake. Occasionally, they also indicate that something not under the user's control has gone wrong. When that happens a repair and recovery operation usually follows very soon thereafter.

extents b-tree The data structure that contains the records of fragmented files. It lists the beginning of each fragment and the size of those fragments. For best results, this tree should be pruned often. To prune it, use a disk optimizer or defragmenter. Fragmented files are hard to recover when you are forced into the manual mode of a recovery operation.

F

file An ordered collection of data that performs a function, represents specific information, or manipulates other files. The integrity of a file is paramount if your system is to operate properly. Missing or added portions will cause the original to perform improperly.

file attributes Indicators that tell your system some important things about each file. They indicate things like whether the file is locked, read-only, or invisible or hidden or was changed since the last backup. Using a good disk editor, you can see the status of the attributes. Changing attributes should be done only when you know what you are changing and what the consequences of the change is.

folder A folder is a collection of files. In most cases, these files will be related in some manner.

font   A font is a single size, style, and weight of a given typeface. Each variation of any of the listed characteristics becomes a different font.

Font/DA Mover   A special application utility that allows you to add or remove fonts and Desk Accessories from your System Folder.

format   There are a number of formats in the computer world. One is the action of preparing a disk for use. This format writes the housekeeping information onto the media. Another format is that of a data file. This format specifies where each type of information is to be placed and how much space it is allowed to occupy. Formatting a disk is basically the same. It lays out what information is to be placed where and how much of the disk's space it is allowed to occupy.

full backup   When all of the information on a disk is copied to another similar media, a full backup has been performed. Making a typed copy of all your text files should not be considered a backup or any type. Making tape or diskette copies of all your hard disk files is backing up your hard disk.

H

hexadecimal   Hex means six and decimal means ten. Together, they identify the number system that uses sixteen characters to represent all of the individual values in the system. The characters used are the decimal digits zero through nine and the letters A through F. The letters are used to represent the values of what would be double digit numbers in the decimal system. That is $A = 10$, $B = 11$, $C = 12$, $D = 13$, $E = 14$, and $F = 15$.

Hierarchical File System (HFS)   A system software feature that lets you organize the information on your disks. The disk or volume contains a number of folders or subdirectories, each of which contain a number of files. These files can be applications or the information generated by applications.

I

incremental backup   An incremental backup differs from a differential backup in that it doesn't make a copy that supersedes the previous copy. Each incremental backup copy is unique and necessary to restore everything to a disk to its current condition. Each increment contains only those things that have been changed since the last full or incremental backup. This differs from the differential in that the differential copies all of the changes since the last full backup each time it is made.

initialization   Initialization is the same as formatting. It prepares the disk with the necessary housekeeping information to permit the recoverable writing of information to its data storage areas.

interleave   Interleaving is the descriptive term used when talking about how the sectors of a track are being read or written to. Normally, the scheme used for a single track is the one used for the entire cylinder. A 1:1 interleave means that the sector numbers follow in order. A 2:1 interleave means that the disks reads or writes one sector and skips the next one. A 3:1 interleave would have two other sectors between each sector that is written or read.

K

kilobyte   Means one thousand bytes. It usually represents a true value of 1,024 bytes. This can be the cause for some minor misunderstandings when it comes to describing capacity or space requirements. A kilobyte also can be represented in binary by the value 0100 0000 0000. 400 in hex has the same value.

L

latency   The average time that the read/write head must wait over the correct track for the correct sector to come into position for reading or writing. This time varies with the speed of disk rotation, the length of the sectors, and the distance from the hub. The term usually seen in descriptions of disk performance is the average latency. There shouldn't be much difference in this value from disk to disk regardless of the manufacturer. The speed of rotation and the location of the tracks has been fixed as has the number of sectors per track.

Local Area Network (LAN)   A group of computers in a limited area connected together for the purpose of sharing resources. The area limitation can be a room or a building. In some cases, adjacent buildings might be included into a very large LAN. When the interconnection goes beyond this point, it usually is referred to as a WAN, or Wide Area Network. One distinctive characteristic of either network is that any of the individual computers can be in continuous communication with any of the other computers in the network.

M

Macintosh File System (MFS)   A single-level file system where there is just the disk and the files. There is no ability to segregate files into small logical groups and then combine the groups into larger logical divisions. This system was used by the original Macintoshes. Most 400K diskettes use this system. Some of the newer utility programs do not support this older file system.

megabyte (Mb)   A megabyte is one thousand kilobytes or 1,024,000 bytes.

Modified Frequency Modulation (MFM)   One of the methods used to record information on hard disks. It has nothing to do with the content or format of the information

modem   A modulator/demodulator is the device that allows the digital information in your computer to be transmitted over the telephone company's wires to another microcomputer or bulletin board service. The modulator, or sender, portion of the modem translates your system's information into a signal that is acceptable to the phone company's wiring and electronics. The demodulator performs the reverse function of translating the phone acceptable signals into something your system can understand.

N

nibble   A nibble is half a byte, or four bits. When converting binary values to hexadecimal, each nibble is equal to a single hex character.

O

overwrite   To overwrite is to place new or different information into the same location where previously recorded information existed. This is the way your new files are able to occupy the space previously taken by files that have been deleted. Floppy diskette initialization also overwrites all of the data storage areas. There also are utility programs that will overwrite areas so that the information that was present cannot be recovered.

P

parallel   There are two commonly used methods of transferring data via cables. The parallel method utilizes a separate wire for each of the bits in a byte, together with some additional wires for control. This allows all of the bits of a single byte to be transferred at one time. The serial method of transfer uses only two wires and places the bits in one line after the other, or serial fashion.

R

random access memory (RAM)   The memory, or temporary storage, chips in a microcomputer are designed to allow access at any point at any time. They allow random access. This is the same type of access available on disks. Tapes do not allow random access. The usually are accessed serially.

read-only memory (ROM)   Your computer doesn't remember anything after the power is turned off. For it to begin operations again when the power is turned on, it requires instructions. These instructions are written into special chips that retain their information without power applied. When you turn the switch on, these instructions are read into the system RAM and are acted upon by the computer. Usually, the extent of these instructions is to perform a self-test to be sure all is well and then to read the instructions found in the system program that resides on the start-up disk.

resource fork   The resource fork is the nonchanging portion of a file. This is normally where the program code of an application can be found. The changeable information is placed in the data fork. This arrangement allows the programmer to customize the same application code for a number of uses without having to recompile all of the code. This also helps the user keep his/her system in order, because each type of fork should contain its own type of information. The utilities described in this book recognize these types and make sure that only these types are there. When things get out of place in a system, it usually crashes. Safe hex should prevent most problems. For those few that it can't prevent, it can cushion the impact.

S

Small Computer System Interface (SCSI)   The name of a set of rules for interconnecting devices to a microcomputer. The Macintosh uses the SCSI (also known as Scuzzy) interface. DOS-based microcomputers (IBM and its clones) use either a parallel or serial interface. IBM has announced its support of the SCSI interface. This will assist in the transfer of information from Macs to PCs.

sector   A sector is defined as that portion of a track that holds 512 bytes of information together, with its address and any error checking code. Each track will have a number of sectors. In some cases, the length of the sectors will vary, while the number per track is constant. Other schemes use uniform sector lengths with a varying number per track. The tracks near the hub have fewer than those near the edge or rim.

seek time   The time it takes the read/write head of your disk drive to move from its present location to the location you have requested. Because this time will be directly proportional to the distance traveled, the value usually seen for comparison is average seek time. This time is used to indicate how quickly the head moves between requested tracks, or cylinders, under normal operating conditions. The other seek time often reported is the track-to-track seek time. This is the length of time it takes the read/write head to move in or out a single track. This value, for a hard disk, is usually many times lower than the average. It also is many times faster than the times posted by a floppy diskette. To see the true differences between disks, you must be sure that you are comparing like numbers to like numbers.

serial   Serial means one after the other. A serial signal can be transmitted using only two conductors. The nearest analogy might be a telegraph signal.

suitcase   Desk Accessory and Font files are held in suitcases. These are special file types that can be moved in and out of the System File as needed. The Font/DA Mover application is used to perform this action. The utility program Suitcase II, described elsewhere, is another means of doing the same thing. It's advantage is that it can create suitcase files that hold a number of other suitcases. This allows you to move special groups of suitcases around as necessary.

T

track   A track is the band around the surface of a disk that is always at the same distance from the center point. The width of this band varies. As technology improves, the width gets narrower, so more bands can be placed within each measured inch of surface as measured along any radius. Tracks are subdivided into sectors and collected into cylinders.

tracks per inch (TPI)   The physical width of each track and the amount of space allowed between each track determine the number of tracks per inch. Older floppy disks have relatively few tracks per inch. Some of the newest hard disks are claiming 600 TPI or more.

transfer rate   The number of bytes per unit of time that can be moved from your disk to your system RAM, or in the reverse direction, is the transfer rate. The value usually is given in kilobytes per second (KPS). This is being replaced with megabytes per second as the hardware and the technology improve. Even higher transfer rates will be possible as soon as the problem of bus speed is overcome. Electrons can move only so fast through the copper conductors. The longer the distance the greater the time required. Long times force low transfer rates.

trojan horse   The descriptive name comes from the pages of Greek mythology. This is a program that looks like it's doing something useful for you while it actually is doing you harm.

A Trojan Horse cannot reproduce, replicate, itself. It must be executed, or run, for the damage to be done. To transfer a Trojan Horse from one system to another, the infected file must be copied or moved to that system and run.

typeface The name given to the shape of a character. Each distinctive set of character shapes usually has a name. Times Roman, Helvetica, Courier, and Geneva are typeface names. They also have styles such as shadow, narrow, italics, etc. Each of these also might come in a number of line weights, light, bold, etc. They also are classified by size. The printer's unit of measure is the "point". There are 72 points in an inch. To fully describe a printed character, you must include the typeface name, style, and weight, as well as the size.

U

undelete When you eliminate a file from a disk by moving it to the Trash Can, you are said to be deleting it. When you use a utility program to retrieve that file from the Trash Can, it is called undeleting the file. This procedure works only as long as the data on the disk has not been overwritten. Overwritten information is lost forever.

upload When you transfer a file or files from your system to another system or service, you upload to that computer.

V

virus A special type of problem code. It must have a host to carry it. It doesn't stand alone like the other problems that can infect a computer. It's other distinctive feature is that it reproduces or replicates itself into other host programs. It is at least as damaging to system operations as any other form of infection. The total amount of damage it does usually is greater because of its capability to reproduce. Once it is in a system, it can spread to any other system under certain conditions much more easily than the others.

volume A disk or diskette or portion thereof that has a separate identity. Large hard disks often are divided, or partitioned, into volumes to make housekeeping easier. Some of these housekeeping tasks are backups, searches, optimization, security, encryption, and compression.

W

worm A stand alone program designed to replicate itself and spread throughout a system or network. It might or might not do damage other than to replicate. The act of replicating can be likened to the increases in a value when subjected to geometric progression. From one comes two, then four, then eight, etc. Each time the first program replicates, all of its children also can. Large portions of a disk or a network of disks can become loaded down with this code. Because it is recognized by the operating system as a valid program, the user will soon see a Disk full error message when there is no reason to expect it.

Index

About the author

I am married and have three children and a grandson. I and my family live in Charlotte, NC. I am an ex-Army officer and Viet Nam veteran. I was born in Chicago, have lived in Arizona and California, as well as in a few foreign countries. (The overseas travel was by government request.)

A machine and mechanical systems designer by profession, I also am a teacher. I have served as a part-time instructor at a local community college and am active in my church congregation. Other teaching experiences in the Army and the Red Cross have helped me to develop an understanding of what students really need to learn a subject. Working with the local AutoCAD Users Group also has confirmed that these needs don't change much from generation to generation.

My illustrated tutorial series of books is an attempt to provide these tools to a wider base of learners. They are an adaptation of my understanding of what a lesson plan should contain. I believe that my philosophy that "there are only two stupid questions in this world" makes it easier for the student to ask questions in order to learn. The stupid questions are those not asked when the answer isn't known and those asked when the answer is known. The first prevents learning; the second wastes time.

I have extended my classroom into the electronic world of telecommunications for the past six years as ELLISCO on DELPHI. As the System Monitor and general assistant to most of the information Providers (IPs), I am available almost every night. Helping users learn how to get the most out of their connect time is as rewarding as helping a new IP learn how to provide users with the best possible information in an easy to use form. DELPHI isn't the largest service available, but in my opinion, it is the best. It's a prejudiced opinion, but I have stuck with it. I am on DELPHI exclusively, so don't look for me on any of the other services.

Good and bad comments are appreciated. I make mistakes, but I don't like them to appear in print. If you see something wrong, write to me in care of TAB Books and we will correct it. If you like what you read, suggest that a friend buy his or her own copy to read. (I've got two kids in college and every extra penny helps.)

For those of you who noticed the dedication, I should explain. Stan Viet was the editor-in-chief of the *Computer Shopper* for many years. He is the man who bought my first article. Ron Powers is the Director of Acquisitions at TAB Books. He bought my first book. I owe these men a debt that I'm not sure I can repay directly. If my thanks mean anything, they have it. In the meantime, I will attempt to pass on what I've learned from them.